INVESTING WITH THE BEST

Other Books by the Author

Stock Market Primer

The Common Sense Way to Stock Market Profits

Psycho-Cybernetics and the Stock Market

INVESTING WITH THE BEST

What to Look For
What to Look Out For
in Your Search for a
Superior Investment Manager

CLAUDE N. ROSENBERG, JR.

JOHN WILEY & SONS

New York • Chichester • Brisbane • Toronto • Singapore

Library of Congress Cataloging in Publication Data:

Rosenberg, Claude N.
  Investing with the best.

  Includes index.

  1. Investment advisers.   2. Investments—Management.
I. Title.   II. Title: Investment manager.
HG4521.R775   1986   332.6   86-1611
ISBN 0-471-83798-9

Printed in the United States of America

10 9 8 7 6 5 4

To all investor clients,
who by and large have deserved better;
and specifically to those who
over the years have expressed confidence
in me or my organization,
who at the very least have
received an honest effort.

FOREWORD

Investing with the Best presents an attractive combination as a book that both fills a crying need and has been written by the right person.

The crying need . . . is the ability to separate the competent from the less competent and the completely ethical from the less ethical investment advisers.

The writer . . . is Claude Rosenberg, who brings his knowledge and insights as a competent, completely ethical investment adviser to the reader. In *Investing with the Best*, Claude shows those of us who entrust investment decisions to others how to overcome such obstacles as:

inadequate (investment) industry standards, which lead to

questionable practices that are very difficult for clients to detect and which leave us vulnerable to false claims.

Claude Rosenberg has set an unusual example of devotion to professionalism. Over the 15 years I've known Claude, he has never stopped improving his approach to the investment process. He takes the time to reflect on the real meaning of his many experiences, always probing for ways to better serve his clients. His dissatisfaction with the mediocre and his quest for the best have helped his clients and earned him the high regard of his business competitors, professional peers, and many friends.

Claude has been successful as one of a very few who has advised others wisely in three investment areas of: growth stocks, bonds, and real estate. One reason for this success is that clients are very important to Claude; clients have always come ahead of his firm's economic interests. His major business participation, Rosenberg Capital Management, has been virtually closed to new accounts for years, refraining from cashing in on its credibility by seeking a plethora of new business. Claude and his partners care much more about something else: being truly professional.

Investing with the Best constitutes the basis for greater success by all investors—particularly those entrusting investments to others. It's fitting that a book geared to helping investment clients has been written by a person who understands what clients should expect and who cares deeply about their well-being.

Claude Rosenberg is an engaging, energetic, modest, and delightful man. He is always learning, growing, and teaching.

Investing with the Best is an extension of this positive person. You will benefit from the knowledge, experience, and advice he offers. The book is honest and down-to-earth and is certain to make an immediate, profound, and very positive difference in your investment behavior.

CHARLES D. ELLIS
GREENWICH ASSOCIATES RESEARCH

PREFACE

There was desperation in the voice at the other end of the telephone.

Although the caller's life was clearly not in danger, his "Will you please—*please*—help me find somebody to handle our investing" conveyed serious frustration.

Oddly enough, the desperate caller was no neophyte to the business world or to success. In fact, he was a reasonably wealthy individual who had recently retired as president of a very prestigious company. He was now a busy consultant who was also contributing his talents as a director of his former company and as a trustee for an important charitable foundation and an equally prominent eastern university.

"I don't know what we should do," he went on to say, "and my cohorts know even less than I. We can't talk the language of either consultants or money managers—and we are obviously on the receiving end of some very fancy marketing persuasion. And by the way," he continued, "I could use some help personally. I've been hounded by brokers, investment bankers, managers, and consultants, and I'm as confused as the institutions I represent about how to invest my funds wisely."

The caller's dilemma was hardly surprising or unusual, but his attitude was. In short, he recognized his and his associates' shortcomings, and he pleaded ignorance of investment management—a field most people know just enough about to persuade themselves they can handle the challenge. Furthermore, he recognized the "hype" prevalent among the money managers hawking their services.

You probably share this individual's frustration. You probably are concerned about your personal investing, and you may be one of many who have either direct or indirect responsibility for funds belonging to others. How do you sort through the confusing array of investing strategies and talents to find the person or firm best equipped to handle your money?

What to do? What to do?

The answer, which exists nowhere else in organized form that I know of, lies in the pages that follow.

CLAUDE N. ROSENBERG, JR.

San Francisco, California
April 1986

ACKNOWLEDGMENTS

Were I a singer and entertainer like the late Maurice Chevalier, I would indeed sing out a "Thank heavens . . ." for the help I received from the many sides of the investment business. Fortunately for me, clients, fellow managers, consultants, investment strategists, and academics asked to read parts or all of the manuscript and were willing to criticize and make helpful suggestions. These inputs, along with some special editorial comments from them and others, helped me immensely with structure, tone, and content.

My very special thanks, therefore, go out to clients Gary Bland (Boeing), Adrian Cassidy (Pacific Telesis), Terry Clifford (Tektronix), Robert Evans (Xerox), Anthony Hall (Bristol-Myers), R. H. (Tad) Jeffrey (Jeflion Investment Co.), Drew Mathieson (Mellon Foundation), Roger Meier (state of Oregon), Arthur Miltenberger (Mellon), Janice Murphy (Pacific Gas & Electric), Robert Norman (Chevron), A. G. (Gus) Olsen (Abbott Labs), L. Guy Palmer (General Motors), Donald W. Phillips (Ameritech), and Rich Reisinger (Tektronix); to consultants George Russell, Charley Ellis, and Mrs. Joyce Linker, and to Professor John G. (Jack)

McDonald of Stanford's GSB; to economists and authors Peter L. Bernstein, Barton Biggs, Harold Ehrlich, and Steven Leuthold; to friendly competitor investment managers Kurt Hauser (Wentworth, Hauser), Robert Kirby (Capital Guardian), Dean LeBaron (Batterymarch), Andy Pilara (Pilara Associates), and J. F. (Jay) Sherrerd (Miller, Anderson & Sherrerd; and to many of my fellow partners at Rosenberg Capital Management.

My sincere appreciation to Angela Haines, Timothy Schwarz, and S. Stuart Swanson, who gave me some good structural inputs early on; to George Davis and Diana Chow Blasi, who made some important contributions; to Della van Heyst of Stanford University, who encouraged me and gave me valuable advice that led me to Susan Wels; and to Susan, who worked like a Trojan to rescue me from the fog that surrounded me after three years of writing, gave me fresh perspective, and helped me bring the project to fruition.

Final, final appreciation goes to someone who fortunately for me can be thanked daily—my wife, Weezy, who bore with me and understood my periodic frustrations heightened by my impatience to get something out that had been burning inside for so long.

Again, to all, my sincere "thank you" for your interest, thoughtfulness, and efforts.

C. N. R.

CONTENTS

INVESTING WITH THE BEST

1 FINDING THE BEST TO INVEST YOUR MONEY

When, lo, as they reached the
mountain-side,
A wondrous portal opened wide,
As if a cavern was suddenly
hollowed;
And the Piper advanced and the
children followed,
And when all were in to the very last,
The door in the mountain-side shut
fast.

Robert Browning
The Pied Piper of Hamelin

Whether you're responsible for a billion-dollar institutional portfolio, oversee a $2 million trust, or simply have $50,000 or $100,000 of your own funds to manage, investing money has never been a more demanding or sophisticated challenge. Wildly fluctuating markets, investors' expectations for high returns, and a huge number of new investment products have dramatically changed the character of the investing game—and made the aid of investment advisers a necessity for most serious players.

Between 1970 and 1984, the amount of money under professional investment management jumped tenfold from approximately $100 billion to $1 trillion, and the number of registered investment advisers rose from 3060 to 9000 (2000 joined the field in 1984 alone). At the same time, however, attempts by industry associations and the Securities and Exchange Commission to make sure those advisers behave responsibly have essentially failed. In fact, the explosively growing field of investment management is rife with questionable practices that make it difficult for even the most sophisticated clients to tell the deceivers from the performers.

As a result, finding the best person or the best organization to invest your money is one of the most important financial decisions you'll ever make. It's also one of the toughest. The right manager for someone else may not be the right manager for you, nor can you reasonably expect to find many objective, or even reliable, sources to help you narrow your choices. You will be bombarded with promotional pitches and inundated with figures, charts, and statistics that seek to sell you on each adviser's services. But where do you turn next?

The sad fact is that too often you cannot even believe what has been presented to you. Despite the billions upon billions of dollars under professional management, consistent standards for presenting past performance records are simply inadequate. In fact, performance results—which should be a most revealing guide for clients—normally pose more questions than they answer. Performance statistics are filled with potential traps, and they are often riddled with dishonesty and deception. As a result, you are left in the uncomfortable position of taking a salesperson's word to evaluate his or her firm's past record. If you could properly analyze some of the promotional tactics used—and abused—by certain investment managers, you would quickly learn how high your chances are of being misled.

Damaging conflicts of interest exist, too. Unfortunately, most investor clients depend on advice or management from individuals or organizations whose compensation benefits significantly from brokerage or other commissions, so that rewards result from an account's *activity,* not its results. While many investment professionals are not motivated selfishly and do serve their clients well, the temptations remain. The onus is decidedly on you, the "buyer," to inform and protect yourself.

Be warned that mistakes can be very costly. You can always fire a manager, sell a mutual fund or terminate a broker relationship, but liquidating costs added to the sum of cumulated investment losses easily mount up. The emotional penalties of poor initial decisions are also considerable.

You—the investing client—may not consider yourself to be like the children of Browning's Pied Piper, but you are hardly safe from similar dangerous temptations to follow the leader blindly. The "investors' graveyard" is strewn with the bones of those who lacked adequate insights into the process of making money through others.

Up to now, there has been a dearth of advice on successful investing through investment managers. The veritable orphan has indeed been the person or organization who entrusts money to others. *Investing with the Best* fills this void. There are no claims that this book will enable you to make money easily, but it will give you numerous practical, profit-directed tools for selecting and then reassessing your manager—tools that investors simply have not had access to before.

Why am I qualified to guide you safely through this investment jungle? For more than 30 years I have been investing successfully for myself and for others, including personal investors and major institutional clients responsible for mutual funds, pension and profit-sharing plans, foundations, and endowments. My investment management firm is responsible for over $5 billion in client funds. And my three previous books—*Stock Market Primer, The Common Sense Way to Stock Market Profits*, and *Psycho-Cybernetics and the Stock Market*—have helped hundreds of thousands of investors make their way through the daunting maze of personal and professional investing. Over and over again, I have observed practices within the investment management industry that make me wince—and that surely can and should be rectified. My goals in writing this book are to show you how to avoid some common pitfalls that threaten you; to help raise investment management standards generally; and to provide you with the practical steps you can take to improve your own investment results.

Just as there is skill involved in making money for yourself, there is skill involved in finding, retaining, and nurturing superior investment management. This book should help you cultivate those skills. After all, you (the client) may not be as proficient at buying and selling securities as the managers you seek, but this book will help you develop an "investment sense"—a perceptiveness about investing that should serve you well in many investing situations you may face over the years. You need not be as technically competent as managers, but the very knowledge this book presents—about investing cycles and styles, about fighting herd instincts, about the emotional side of investing, about developing sensitivities and certain protections against people who sell investment "products"—should prove valuable in all types of decisions likely to confront you.

Organized into three parts, this book provides a step-by-step guide to securing successful investment management. Part 1 lays the foundation. Whether you're responsible for a $500 million corporate portfolio or personally investing $100,000, Part 1 will give you valuable tools and behind-the-scenes insights into investing and the investment management world. You'll learn how recent changes in investment markets have created new problems and challenges for investors. You'll also learn how to assess your own investment "personality" and recognize your tolerance for risk. After all, one obstacle to clients' success is often . . . the client himself! Whether you are an individual or an institutional client, you can be a hindrance to your own investment returns. This is a problem that remains largely ignored because clients often possess bad habits without recognizing them and because it is hardly in a manager's best interests to point out his clients' shortcomings.*

---

*As critical as I am of many investment manager practices, I cannot resist mentioning that Brown-

An interesting article in the *Harvard Business Review* entitled "Rate Yourself as a Client"[†] illustrates this point. Though the article was not directed to investment clients, it concluded aptly:

> Few of us . . . have thought of ourselves in terms of how good we are as clients . . . though we probably give ourselves pretty good marks. That's half the trouble—it's one of those private activities like selection interviewing or sexual intercourse which, since we never put them on public display or try them out in competition, we can always kid ourselves we're pretty good at

Part I also teaches you:

How to improve your chances of selecting a winner to manage your money, with specific advice on how to set realistic guidelines for yourself and your adviser, avoid false expectations, and distinguish good investment decision making from weak approaches

How to differentiate among the wide-ranging investment cycles and styles you are certain to encounter, with specific advice on how to benefit from these cycles and styles rather than being whipsawed by them, as so many investors are

That you may not need a manager at all!

Parts 2 and 3 provide a wealth of helpful advice and guidelines. These two sections show you what to look for and look out for in investment advisers.

Part 2 takes you into the inner sanctum of the investment management business, a business that Robert Evans, pension director of Xerox Corporation, describes as "one which is quick to criticize others, while being perhaps the worst-managed business in the country." You'll discover:

---

ing's Pied Piper lured away the unsuspecting children only after the adults (his "clients") refused to pay him as promised for ridding the town of Hamelin of its rats!

†Anthony Jay, "Rate Yourself as a Client," *Harvard Business Review*, July–August, 1977.

Certain very questionable, previously unpublicized practices used by some advisers

How to spot both dishonest and unrepresentative performance records

How to assess the risks that managers have taken with the funds you control

How to handle the delicate subject of fees—to ensure that you get what you pay for when you employ a manager (or invest in a pooled investment vehicle, such as a mutual fund)

Part 3 shows you how to select and manage your manager by developing a successful working relationship. Again, the advice is specific—you'll learn:

How to evaluate compensation levels and other factors affecting the stability of manager organizations

How to check personal references of staff members as well as a firm's reputation in the industry

That luck can affect an adviser's investment results

How to distinguish this fleeting influence from more telling qualities

This book spares no punches, and advice is plentiful. Numerous Client Guides are provided, including handy questionnaires and checklists to help you make and then reinforce your appraisals of managers. These guides are supplemented by important Manager Queries—specific penetrating questions for you to pose to potential managers to help you separate the strong from the weak, the able from the less competent.

The audience for this book includes:

1. Institutional clients, including all officers, trustees, and directors who are interested in, or ultimately responsible for, the investable assets of their organizations.

2. Taxable investors with sufficient assets to warrant individualized attention either from investment managers or from brokers who operate as advisers do.

3. Investors contemplating entrusting funds to others, including many who need help in selecting mutual funds. While the book is pointed to clients who have more active associations with their investment managers than mutual funds provide, more than two-thirds of the pages (Chapters 2 through 7, plus 9, 12, and 15) prepare fund clients with unusual and valuable insights and advice.

4. Investment managers, brokers, and consultants. Alas, my hope is that the investment advisory industry will benefit from greater scrutiny and demands from clients.

Much of the advice of the book is so fundamental that it applies to a broad spectrum of investing decisions you will make. The Client Guides, along with the sensible general investing advice provided, should make you a more knowledgeable and successful investor. The book, therefore, will help you place your money in the right places at the right times by yourself, but it will be particularly useful if you are seeking the same wise decisions with the help of others. *Investing with the Best* will make those of you who are do-it-yourself investors far better judges of other investors who are competing against you, and the book will enable those of you who are investment clients or slated to become such clients to be far better judges of those people you hire to manage your funds. Remember—the rallying cry of this book is that you *can* influence and improve your investment results. It should provide the defense you need to avoid the costliest mistakes and the offense necessary to succeed in making money either on your own or through others.

(Note: Whereas once upon a time the investment business was practically the exclusive purview of males, thank goodness the barriers have been broken. Today, numerous outstanding female analysts, portfolio managers, and other professionals exist. Therefore, I hope my reference to managers in the masculine throughout the book is understood to be simply editorial shorthand. In every case, "he" means "he or she"; "his" means "his or her"; "him" means "him or her"; and so on.)

1

THE SECRETS OF SUCCESSFUL INVESTING— ON YOUR OWN OR THROUGH OTHERS

2

INVESTING HAS CHANGED— AND YOU MAY HAVE TO CHANGE BECAUSE OF IT

Presume not that I am the thing I was.
William Shakespeare
Henry IV

Investing has always been dynamic. Stock and bond prices change constantly, as do definitions of quality. Similarly, the trade-offs between losing and making money (labeled "risk—reward prospects" within investment circles) flutter like feathers in a windstorm.

Since change is so normal, it may seem pointless to suggest that investors may have to alter their ways because of it. Investing *is* different than it used to be, however—and investors who aim to improve must reckon with the changes that have occurred.

HOW HAS INVESTING CHANGED?

Many investors have lost touch with reality. They are confused about what they should reasonably expect from their investments and therefore uncertain what to demand from those to whom they entrust their money.

One reason for this is the general state of economic affairs that has developed since the mid-1970s. Fears of economic collapse, of depression, and of its mirror image, rampant inflation, have become more legitimate than at any time since the end of World War II.

Another source of trouble emanates from a major shift in common stock investing. Investors have changed their focus from a long-standing concentration on obtaining current income to a greater concern with the future trend of that income and, most particularly, with the prospects for capital appreciation.

From the 1930s through World War II and into the early postwar period, the economic times spawned investment habits that emphasized survival. The outlook for many businesses was tenuous, and most investors limited their hopes by concentrating on and demanding high current income from equities. As a result, *for every year from the Depression through 1958, common stocks offered more dividend yield than the income available from bond interest rates.** After this, investors

---

*Over the 29 years from 1930 to 1958, stock yields exceeded bond yields by as little as .54 percent, and by as much as 4.87 percent, with the average being 2.37 percent.

began concentrating more heavily on capital growth possibilities again. Prospects for growth—the projection of companies' earnings-per-share growth leading to payment of higher dividends and this combination leading to higher stock prices— supplanted the emphasis on current income. From 1959 to 1967, common stock yields averaged about 1 percent *below* bond yields, and since then the trend of sharply rising interest rates has led to higher and higher current income from bonds versus stocks. By 1986 the average disparity was over 6 *percent*. This significantly lower income available from equities versus bonds reflects strong expectation of higher stock prices in the future. After all, if the current dividend yield from ABC stock is 3 percent versus 12 percent annual interest from a bond, an investor must be counting on something exceptional happening to ABC's market price and dividend stream to overcome this 9 percent lower annual income.

The dramatic shift in income from, and expectations for, stocks versus bonds implies that the risks of common stock ownership have increased. After all, if investors perceive that little or no growth is likely again, common stocks are vulnerable to major slides. The optimist might argue that growth is assured. Or he could argue that bonds are simply too cheap and that a sharp rise in bond prices will bring their yields down far enough to approximate stock yields again. Without such a surge in bonds, stocks require substantial capital appreciation to produce competitive returns— *and this demand for capital growth has led to greater need for investment advice.*

When income was the major focus, many more investors felt they could handle the management job adequately themselves (simply by scanning available dividend yields and selecting stocks accordingly). As bird-in-the-hand income became less important, many do-it-yourself investors converted to clients seeking professional help to catch two-in-the-bush capital growth.

This trend, then, created the following scenario:

1.   Heavy emphasis on capital appreciation has led to more volatile markets and to greater swings in investment results. Volatility of results has led to greater confusion among clients about which managers they should hire, retain, or fire.

2.   The investment advisory business has changed in character and approach. Advisers are no longer mainly shepherds of a slow-moving flock; they are hired mainly to create capital gains. Clients recognize that this requires more talent, which has led to more promises being made to them. The need and the promises have led to sharply higher management fees, which create an additional cost burden for clients to offset.

3.   Investor expectations have become more grandiose. Performance figures, once seldom emphasized—much less documented—with any semblance of exactness (other than by mutual funds), have suddenly become the object of client worship.

4.   Emphasis on capital growth has complicated the job of performance calculation. Confusion, including significant deception, has occurred in performance presentation.

5.   Institutions have become a dominant force in the stock market. Many pension and profit-sharing plans once held small percentages of their portfolios in common stocks, but this has changed. In 1958, when American Telephone announced it was allocating up to *10 percent* of its pension assets to common stocks, it was considered daring. In contrast, corporations today consider 50 percent representation in stocks a bare minimum figure, with many allowing up to 75 percent to 80 percent for equity ownership. This, too, has created client nervousness. After all, investors are bound to be more nervous about performance when they have one-half to three-quarters of their funds in a given asset than when they have only 10 to 25 percent.

Furthermore, the tax-free nature of most institutional money means that fewer inhibitions to trading exist. Institutions do not consider selling for tax-loss purposes as do taxable accounts, but institutions have no reluctance to take capital gains. In some cases, as with pension funds, realizing gains can be more beneficial than letting them "ride." As a consequence, institutional activity in the stock market, which once constituted a small percentage of trading, accounted for an estimated 60 to 70 percent of daily activity in 1984 and 1985.

Turnover of portfolio holdings has ballooned, and this, like any trading activity, is bound to be costly. One study of college and university endowment funds typifies the current frenzy: Turnover of stocks held by these investors jumped from 17.4 percent of portfolio value in 1975 to

53.5 percent in 1984. (Bond turnover went from 9.6 to 42.0 percent.)

The picture is clear. The immense size of institutional money, with its freedom to trade and its greater concentration on capital appreciation, has led to burgeoning portfolio turnover—which has produced wilder and wilder days in the stock market. Daily swings of 10 to 30 points in the Dow Jones Industrial Average (DJIA) are far more common than they were, and trading volume has skyrocketed.* Volatility can be treacherous, with earnings disappointments of mere pennies per share causing daily declines of 10–20% in individual stocks.

6. Fixed-income securities (bonds, preferred stocks, etc.) have undergone a dramatic upheaval. Once considered by many to be an asset to be bought for income-producing purposes and not to be sold unless credit (un-)worthiness suggested income wouldn't be paid, bonds and their counterparts experienced drastic depreciation in market price. Declining bond prices existed in over two-thirds of the years from 1952 to mid-1982. Severe portfolio losses were incurred by those (unfortunately, the vast majority) who followed a buy-and-hold bond strategy. Thus, bonds changed from being dull but secure to being volatile and usually painful. This has led to an altered view of how these securities should be considered, which has led to active fixed-income management and most of the same performance and assessment problems that equities now face.

INVESTOR REACTIONS

Investors have responded to the new conditions by seeking more sophistication in their planning and more short-term assessment of their results. This attention is decidedly superior to neglect, but it has not been

---

*Comparisons become startling when you consider a description of the (in-) action that persisted in the stock markets of the 1930s and 1940s and the relatively low volume of trading even through the early 1970s. An acquaintance of mine who had weathered the difficulties of being a stock broker through the 1930s, 1940s, and early 1950s pointed to a (mechanically) stalled stock ticker tape in 1963 and said: "This will shock you, but I can remember so many days from 1930 to 1950 when minutes —no, hours—would pass with precious little movement in the ticker tape. And it wasn't because of mechanical difficulties, either! A 'print' of a 500-share transaction was considered a 'block trade bonanza.' "In contrast, average trading volume on the New York Stock Exchange was 91.2 *million* shares per day in 1984. On a few occasions, volume actually exceeded 200 million shares (with a high of 236 million traded on August 3, 1984). Also, a very active options market (which arbitrages against securities on the NYSE) exists.

without significant problems. Many client organizations have entrusted people not necessarily au courant with investing in publicly traded securities with large responsibilities in this very same area. In many instances, their tenure is only 2 or 3 years, which means: (1) that, if this role is to enhance their career path, they may be tempted to demand faster results than should be expected from investing; and (2) that, just around the time they become sophisticated judges of investment management talent, they are off to another post in the organization.

Furthermore, even those who are well trained often have to report to high-ranked committees that typically lack investment sophistication and, equally dangerous, fail to recognize this deficit. As David Feldman, director of the world's largest pension fund (AT&T), said to me one day: "Committee or board members readily admit that they know nothing about #5 switching machine, but practically everybody has an investment view or bias. A little bit of knowledge is a dangerous thing."

Hence, committees often make emotional or weakly conceived policy decisions, frequently overruling their better-informed designate.

Many institutions have sought outside help, and the academic community and consultants have stepped in. While many worthwhile methodologies have been developed to aid in the assessment of managers and performance results, the services have often been as inexact as the investment management business that they claim to assess. In many cases, the consultants overemphasize near-term performance results and actually encourage overreaction to short-term disappointments (especially where they are paid more for manager searches than for more passive monitoring). Some quarter-by-quarter "horse races" have developed, and many clients (and certain consultants) have embraced a "what have you done for me lately?" approach. As a fellow manager said to me one day: "The performance scramble has created a pack of 'numbers jockeys' who are constantly creating dishonest past performance records which are about as reliable as predictors as the racing form!"

The resulting confusion has produced expectations and actions by clients and managers that are highly destructive to both. A fairly typical example occurred with our firm. We had been chosen to manage a portion of a pension fund of a very prestigious and successful U. S.

company. Like many other managers, we have been careful to compete for new business only where we perceive the likelihood of solid long-term relationships. This means finding clients with whom we have the right chemistry, which includes ascertaining that their expectations are realistic. Are they willing to give their manager sufficient time to prove his proficiency? Are they seeking a healthy longer-term relationship?

In this case, the indications were positive. Fine company, good people, reasonable expectations. You can imagine the shock, therefore, when at our first official client meeting the following statement was made by the person directly responsible for pensions: "This past year has been a poor one for our investment managers. Only one of our seven managers beat the market. I guess we're going to have to shake things up. I'd better drop a few managers and look for replacements!"

This statement typifies one of the changes in client attitudes that has complicated investing today. *Whereas management results were considered too casually prior to the 1970s, the numbers are often accorded too much importance today.* Dr. Peter Dietz, one of the country's leading experts on performance analysis, comments wisely on the "many decision makers who place great emphasis on the niceties of quantitatively defined results. Blind use of performance numbers can lead to erroneous conclusions and poor decisions."

Certainly our client had cause for disappointment. Certainly he should have understood why six of the seven underperformed. But in this case he was oblivious to the fact that all seven had dramatically overperformed for him for a number of years and that this particular year was the first in many which professional managers as a group experienced results below the Standard & Poor's (S&P) index. Instead of factoring in past qualities and assessing trends, he arbitrarily assumed an "ax" was in order.

Since our firm had managed assets for only part of that year, we were not included in his survey. His statements definitely signaled, however, that the account had less scope than we had thought. Later actions confirmed the client's quick reaction. Three managers, all recognized as fine investors and all of whom had produced excellent results for the company prior to this year, were fired. The individual vented his frustration—he used the George Steinbrenner approach of terminating competent managers because of short-term disappointments, despite prior winning seasons.

Trigger-finger reactions, such as this, tend to be self-destructive. Fear of failure is commonplace in the investment arena, something good managers learn to overcome. Threatened quick client retribution, however, only magnifies the obstacle of fear managers face in making the best decisions.

Managers' worries about being fired for "poor cause" produce other negative responses injurious to both parties. The less secure a manager feels—the more he "hears footsteps"—the more likely he is to protect his business by increasing his clientele. Obviously, the more accounts he handles and the less discriminating he is about the types of those accounts, the less time he has for attention to his major responsibility: decision making. Managers possess the same propensities to grow as other businesses; they hardly need additional incentives to justify expansion, which is so often detrimental to clients.

None of this is to suggest that a client shouldn't question at all times whether his investment management can be improved. Assessment and reassessment are continuing responsibilities, and the sensible approach to this discipline is the basic thesis of this book. The point is that the decision to fire should not be made without serious reflection. *There will always be managers available with better records. No one organization will remain on top year after year; all will experience years when they fall below the average. Clients who shift from an excellent manager who has just gone through an inevitable below-average period to one who has just had a "hot hand" court the danger of selling low and buying high.*

Too many clients have done exactly that (bought high and sold low). Too many have shifted managers at precisely the wrong times; too many have shifted money from one type of asset to another in similarly unproductive (and expensive) ways. Figure 2.1, for example, depicts the absolutely horrible timing of pension fund cash flows into common stocks over the past 28 years. Notice how the largest investments have been made near the end of up market cycles and the lowest capital infusions have occurred at the market's low points. As indicated, this inverse relation-

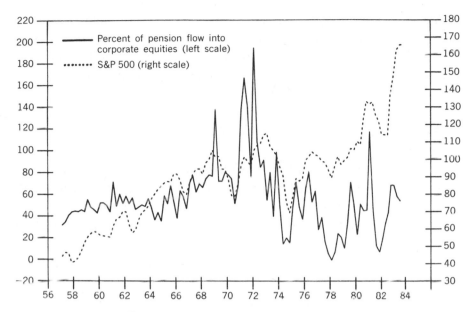

Figure 2.1. Equity investments by pension funds.

ship has also existed for styles of investment managers hired and fired.

Clients' quickness to react and managers' paranoia about the time they have to produce mark a very significant and potentially very costly trend in investment management. As *Institutional Investor* magazine points out, both absolute and opportunity costs are a significant result of managerial changes. Transition/switching costs, the magazine states, are potentially large:

> It's easy to see why. On the equity side, the rule of thumb is that commissions and market-impact costs together run in the vicinity of 1 to 2 percent of the total value of stocks being liquidated. If the sale involves highly illiquid stocks, however, those costs are more likely to be in the 15 to 20 percent range. On top of that are the transaction fees that many master trust banks levy, which amount to between $15 and $25 per purchase or sale. Quips one pension officer, "Let's just say that total transaction costs can amount to an arm and a leg and several other body parts, too." (July 1984, p.116)

Although a horse race atmosphere is not totally pervasive (there are many patient, understanding, and mature clients, just as there are managers who can handle the fears of being fired too abruptly), current investing attitudes are generally too reactive for the clients' welfare.

CAN CONSULTANTS RESOLVE THE PROBLEMS?

Can outside, well-trained consultants bring sense to the scene? Truth be known, the number of highly qualified consultants is amazingly small, especially considering the $1 trillion of institutional funds being managed. Many consultants recommend firms without so much as a visit to manager offices or without knowing the people involved. Many prepare lengthy questionnaires and yet never take the crucial step of double-checking managers' responses. As with investment advisers, charlatan consultants exist, including some who possess little or no investment sophistication. Furthermore, potential conflicts of interest exist in many aspects of consulting, most of which go unrecognized by clients. Consultants do not normally share the same fiduciary responsibility as managers or clients, and there is no one qualitatively or quantitatively measuring these "measurers." Consultants justifying their existence often recommend more rapid turnover of managers than would normally be the case. They too often sympathize with the disappointments of investment committees rather than take an unpopular stand. The "shared disappointment" and encouragement to terminate are especially likely if the consultant didn't choose the manager under fire. And many consultants work especially closely with certain advisers on a "you grease my palm, I'll grease yours" referral-for-referral basis. Anyone relying on others for manager selection should ascertain whether any payments or commissions have been or will be paid by would-be managers. There may not be any harm in the arrangement, but you (the client) should know enough to determine whether one recommendation or another is likely to be biased by self-interest. To be safe, you should ask both your consultant and prospetive managers how the introducing party will be compensated.

In a personal letter to me, Donald W. Phillips, director of investment management for Ameritech, succinctly emphasized the risks of dealing with consultants. Phillips said:

> Consultants are too often like brokers, motivated to act contrary to the interest of their clients. Although effective use of objective and informed consultants can provide invaluable aid to clients, the more common occurrence is either ineffective use or biased, self-motivated consultants. The process can be like letting a brokerage house manage your money and trade exclusively with themselves.

My response is a resounding "amen."

Well-trained, objective consultants should (and do) help a lot, but this industry is in need of the same kind of upgrading that the investment management business so sorely needs.

CONCLUSIONS

Investing *has* changed, and quite substantially. A vicious circle exists. Volatility, risk, and a plethora of confusing inputs are breeding nervousness; nervousness is breeding further confusion; and the combination of nervousness and confusion is breeding client and manager actions that are potentially destructive. For you to succeed, you need to understand how to make your way through the investment jungle. What follows should provide you with a map through this jungle to a far more desirable destination.

3

KNOW YOUR
INVESTOR
SELF

"I'm very brave generally,"
he went on in a low voice, "only
today I happen to have a headache."
Tweedledee in Lewis Carroll's
Through The Looking Glass

Investing very wisely demands actions that most investors have never seriously considered before. You may think, for example, that you need only find a good manager and let him "run" with your money. But this can be dangerous. No matter whom you hire, your probabilities for success hinge on *your investing being compatible with your (very) particular financial character*.

Your financial character consists of two parts: your financial strength and your investment "personality." The first, the strength requirement, is obvious. Unless you are a speculator willing to risk inordinate amounts of capital, you know it makes sense to invest only in amounts that will: (1) allow you to weather comfortably some inevitable disappointing periods; and (2) allow sufficient time for your investments to flourish. What is less obvious is the crucial consideration of how money, investing, and financial responsibility create *personality* traits that greatly influence—*but that normally hamper*—investment results. I have seen many examples of investors who understood their financial positions very well but who were oblivious to their tendencies "under fire" to behave foolishly—and often in ways opposite to what their financial positions dictated. Neglecting consideration of your "personality" entails more than monetary risk, however. It endangers one of the most important goals of investing: *peace of mind*.

YOUR FINANCIAL STRENGTH

Knowing how much money you have is only part of understanding your financial wherewithal. You need an understanding of *your financial staying power*, which you can achieve by answering the following questions:

1.   What is your chief source of income, and how stable is it? The nature of your investing, for example, may hinge on how important your day-to-day involvement is in your income-producing activities and how dependent your income is on unique skills or special circumstances. If you are a surgeon, for example, your income may be large and predictable today, but your future income will depend on your personal involvement,

which obviously holds uncertainties. Many organizations possess similar sensitivities. They may depend on the close involvement of one or two key individuals or on certain conditions—such as a single source of supply or demand that is likely to be fickle.

2.   How strong are the assets that constitute your financial condition? Is your balance sheet very strong? Is it liquid? How much debt do you have? In short, how vulnerable are you to financial squeezes, such as hikes in interest rates?

3.   What are your cash flow needs and your liabilities now and in the future? Needless to say, you need to match these with your income and asset projections.

4. What economic conditions or specific industries affect you most, and how should their effects and performance outlook influence your investing? For example, if you or your company are in the steel business, shouldn't your pension fund forgo heavy exposure to common stocks that reflect the same less attractive business characteristics of that industry (such as high labor content, sensitivity to the business cycle, foreign competition, exposure to autos and heavy industry, etc.)? Investment managers who favor companies with these characteristics are likewise suspect for you. It is disturbing, however, how few clients even consider these important factors. Many corporations give little or no thought to them, and nonprofit organizations are often totally unrealistic about their situations. For example, many colleges and universities, faced with nagging operating deficits even during general economic prosperity—and with great vulnerability to deep recessions—have too often chosen managers and portfolio strategies that unfortunately duplicate those risks and do not protect them adequately against potential losses.

The important thing is to look squarely at *present and future strengths and vulnerabilities* and to form a realistic investment strategy around this profile. Although it is tempting to count on favorable conditions continuing down the road, it is dangerous to structure an investment plan totally around this assumption. Such an approach is like playing Russian roulette. Negative shifts in economic and investing conditions as well as personal circumstances have occurred and no doubt will again.

I particularly caution you against managers who claim they can place you in high-risk investments and at the same time shield you from losses. It is very unlikely that they can in fact avoid the "bullets" that may threaten your financial structure. Do not think, for example, that you or your manager can opportunistically trade in and out of weak or cyclical investments as the investing environment changes. Only a small percentage of investors have been able to do this successfully, and the costs of failing can be frighteningly high.

This is not to insist that there are perfect "formulas" for investing or that individuals or organizations apparently in similar positions should invest identically. Less stable entities can at times justify taking bold risks. By contrast, extraordinarily profitable entities should often invest very conservatively. It is mainly poor assessment of investment risks and an organization's financial character that can produce dire results. For example, marginal companies sometimes incur high risks in their aim for the highest investment returns for their pension portfolios, on the theory that the potential payoff justifies the risk and that, in the worst case, the federal government will bail out beneficiaries if the company fails.[*] But, in fact, if investment returns falter and alarm the company's actuary, pension costs would very likely rise to compensate for anticipated losses. And extra pension expenses—added to portfolio losses—could actually hasten the demise of the company itself.

So . . .

TO HEDGE OR NOT TO HEDGE, THAT IS THE QUESTION!

Appraising your financial strength solves only part of the puzzle. Many other variables have to be considered, most dealing with your ability to cope with negative conditions.

It is crucial to decide whether and to what extent you should counterbalance and offset your financial position. Should you own investments

---

[*]Through the Pension Benefits Guarantee Corporation.

that are like or unlike your "wealth source"? And to what degree? To answer this requires that you . . .

KNOW YOUR INVESTMENT PERSONALITY

Investing is obviously filled with surprises, some of which can be avoided and some of which cannot. One important way to mitigate surprise is to understand *before investing* how you are likely to react to the very human *but inhibiting* reactions of fear, envy, greed, anger, worry, and remorse. Specifically, you need to make honest appraisals of your goals, your ability to take risks, your patience levels, and, perhaps most important, your tolerance for pain. Then you need to communicate these personality traits to your manager, who is truly at a disadvantage in achieving your goals without such input from you.

Although a great part of your manager's performance can be attributed to his investment abilities, you as the client can significantly influence results. Farfetched as it may seem, the client/manager association is not unlike the relationship of a homeowner and an interior decorator. If you give no input on the look you desire for your living room, the end result will be totally the product of your decorator —and it is likely that you will not be completely comfortable with the results. On the other hand, if you hire a decorator and describe certain significant preferences (particularly your dislikes), the final product should reflect your tastes and needs. It may not qualify for the cover of *Architectural Digest*, but it stands a better chance of being *right for you*. As with decorating, the ideal formula for investing combines your basic desires and the "decorator's" (your adviser's) skills.

Perhaps a better analogy comes from Roger S. Meier, chairman of the state of Oregon's retirement funds and an especially astute personal investor. Meier suggests that being candid about your investment personality

> Is similar to providing a doctor one of his most helpful diagnostic tools— your medical history. Without proper inputs, without explaining your

investing self to a manager, there will be inconsistencies which are bound
to be detrimental to results.

Unfortunately, however, client directives are often vague, erratic, and
contradictory. What seems a logical and comfortable strategy to clients
under one set of circumstances (as when investment markets are very
positive) too often becomes instantly unacceptable under other conditions. It is also very "human"—if unrealistic—for clients to desire the best
of all worlds from their investments—that is, to wish for and expect the
highest return with the lowest risk. As Robert Kirby, chairman of Capital
Guardian, says: "Everybody talks about setting realistic objectives, but
down deep the goals are the same for all: To get the highest possible total
return." Kirby is saying that clients too often expect the unrealistic: They
want big upside when conditions are favorable, ignoring the fact that a
manager's posture to achieve such upside normally exposes the client to
larger downside when conditions weaken. Practical-thinking investors
subjugate return aspirations to the investing facts of life: You tend to get
what you bargain for; or, said another way, rewards and risk run fairly
parallel over time. (This investing reality is expressed in the adage
imploring investors to "choose between eating well and sleeping well.")

Moreover, typical reactions to money and investing can particularly
inhibit *client* representatives responsible for other people's (not their
personal) funds. Although some people take greater risks, most individuals react far more cautiously when others' funds are their responsibility.
Legislation, such as ERISA (Employees Retirement Income Security Act
of 1974), and the implications of the legal term *fiduciary* tend to magnify
such conservative tendencies. A fine adage for the future might be:
"When people condition their opinions by emphasizing that they have
their 'fiduciary hats on,' watch out—good investment thinking is about
to fly out the window!" Client representatives who have to report to
others, and in many cases whose careers depend on the fruits (or
lemons!) of hired managers, too often concentrate on "protecting their
posteriors" and exhibit too much caution.

While concern over your fellow human being's financial well-being is
commendable, and concern over your personal future is understandable,

extreme caution has seldom been conducive to very successful investing. Just as demanding too much is counterproductive, the hesitancy and lack of imagination that accompany apprehension and negative thinking are poor investing characteristics. Banks that invested accounts mainly in low-yielding government bonds for many years after World War II are sad examples of such an approach; fortunately for the owners of these assets, certain courts have ruled that extreme caution, like extreme risk taking, can be negligent.

UNDERSTANDING THE INVESTING PERSONALITY OF A GROUP

In fact, groups of all sorts face significant obstacles to successful investing. These can include the difficulties of reconciling the differing investing tendencies of all the individuals involved in investment decisions, possible domination by one or two top officers, and the varying levels of sophistication within a group, not to mention the "albatross" of committee decision making! As Yale psychology professor Irving Janis stated in his book, *Groupthink*, the complicated problems of group decision making (even when intelligent, well-intentioned persons are involved) often lead to bad judgments and negative results. Two heads may be better than one, but too many heads too often lead to mediocrity or worse.

Remember also that if the person directly responsible for investments has an attitude or philosophy that does not match that of the body to which he reports, investment strategy is open to dangerous inconsistencies. An example of such inconsistency occurred with a manager friend in the mid-1970s. His client had assigned its pension fund investment responsibility to a particular financial officer who basically didn't like the stock market. He told his investment managers precisely this and he constantly implored them to invest conservatively. "We just don't want to lose a lot of money," he warned constantly. During the poor stock market years of 1973 and 1974, he was delighted with certain of his managers who were fortunate enough to recognize economic problems that badly affected equity (and fixed-income) prices. These managers sold stocks and raised considerable cash prior to the market's biggest declines, and they lost very little money while other investors experienced a temporary but traumatic depreciation of capital. As a result, he praised them and stated often: "We're more concerned about asset declines than about missing some upside—keep up the good work."

The only trouble was that the company's chairman of the board was a confirmed long-term investor with great confidence in equities. He had been through poor markets before and helped set an equity exposure in the pension fund with the knowledge that some bleak periods would exist. When the stock market recovered sharply in 1975, those with extensive cash suddenly "underperformed." They went from being heroes to looking terribly pedestrian, and when the performance results hit his desk he was amazed to find what little share of the advance his portfolios had experienced. He voiced his displeasure to his deputy, who, instead of arguing for a look at combined results of the 1973–1974 debacle and the 1975 bonanza, took the approach of blaming the managers. By 1976, he had fired them, feigning almost total loss of memory of his pleas for conservatism. *Both* the chairman and the financial officer were, of course, to blame. No consistency of investment objectives was demanded; the company simply didn't know what sort of investor it intended to be, and certainly its managers couldn't know, either. While the example doesn't indicate that much was lost by the client, the ensuing changes were actually quite costly; the company incurred the expenses of a total restructuring of its account (estimated expense: 2 to 4 percent)— and its shift to managers whose stocks had just risen sharply led to ultimate underperformance of another 10 to 15 percent within the next 2 years. Even if the company moves hadn't proved so costly, it's not a very good example of how to run a business—or an investment fund.

Even without wide disparities in investing philosophies, individuals responsible for other people's monies face high barriers. They have to deal with the ordinary obstacles to good investing. And they may have to struggle with the extremely difficult task of discerning the investment personalities of numerous other people. It's hard enough to understand yourself as an investor; it is even more difficult to anticipate how a group, often including people not well known to you, will react to different circumstances. So there is a real challenge involved.

If you are a director, trustee, or officer of any entity with money being managed, perhaps you have to set the wheels in motion. (Nothing is as effective as having the chief executive officer do it.) Thrash out your organization's true investing personalities and business vulnerabilities. Only then can you arrive at policies and actions that will be realistic and consistent. Only then can asset mix and manager choice be truly reflective of your institution's investment character.

If the top officers or directors will not insist on a penetrating financial and personality appraisal, then the person with direct assignment for the particular funds should force the question. The problem here is that he is usually a rung or so down the corporate ladder and may not wish to risk encountering difficulties in convincing his superiors—including perhaps a full board of directors—to enter into an appropriate appraisal.

SOLVING THE PROBLEM

To solve the personality problems affecting investment decisions, organizations—like personal investors—need to *assess themselves as individuals*. Do you have the high-growth personality of most 30-year-olds? The income and security needs of most 80-year-olds? The conservative requirements of a 40-year-old salaried worker? Or the bolder, more flexible objectives of a 40-year-old successful businessperson?

This judgment has to be accompanied by the very pertinent question: *Can you act your financial age?* You may be equivalent to a 40-year-old successful businessperson who has few financial pressures and no urgent need for income or near-term capital gains—but will you behave as the patient long-term investor that this category suggests? It is to the benefit of you and your manager to be certain there is a consistency between your description of your needs and your likely actions. In other words, you must be sure that you will not in fact react impatiently and conservatively to the carrying out of your long-term, high-growth goals. If you do respond this way, you should expect conservative results regardless of your stated intentions.

It is also important to determine how *unconventional* you can be as an investor. Dean LeBaron, president of Batterymarch Financial Management, hypothesizes that opportunities exist for creative investors because of what he notes are the follow-the-pack tendencies of agents, such as investment managers, trustees, or a company's pension fund representative. Some very good investment decisions are recognized but not followed solely because of the agent's position. "The guiding principle seems to be that it is better to make a little money conventionally than to run even the smallest risk of losing a lot unconventionally," says LeBaron. There *is* money to be made by being ahead of the crowd, and you should force an analysis of your capability to act contrary to obvious trends. Without this analysis, you stand to be on the wrong side of LeBaron's agency theory.

Whether you're acting for yourself personally or representing an organization where investment judgments are made by a group, you must work to understand your various investment motivations *before choosing an investment manager*. What you want is what has been preached here: an honest self-analysis of yourself and each group member, including personality "leanings," and an analysis of your or your organization's financial wherewithal. Once these factors have been brought out into the open, you may have to strain to force agreement on an investment approach, but it will be worth it. After all, if you cannot decide these issues personally or agree among yourselves before hiring others, you cannot expect maximum compatibility with your manager after the hiring.

Understanding your financial wherewithal and your investor personality equals knowing your investor self (and heightening your chances for success!)

Client Guide 1 is an easy-to-use questionnaire for any individual, family group, or organization wishing to know more about itself and wishing to construct realistic, consistent, and well-stated investment goals.

The questionnaire must be filled out privately and candidly (and in some isolated cases, anonymously) by those directly or indirectly responsible for investment funds. The wording is intended for a group, but the guide is equally pertinent for your personal investing.

CLIENT GUIDE 1
The Rosenberg "Know Your Investor Self and Your Investment Objectives" Questionnaire

My view of our organization[a] is	"Weak - - - - - - - - Strong"				
1. Our *current* financial condition is	1	2	3	4	5
2. Our *future* "ability to pay" our obligations is likely to be	1	2	3	4	5
3. Our risk-taking ability is generally	1	2	3	4	5
4. Our risk-taking attitude is generally	1	2	3	4	5
5. Our past experience in "buying low and selling high" has been:					
a. In shifting assets	1	2	3	4	5
b. In directing cash flows to various assets	1	2	3	4	5
c. In making manager changes	1	2	3	4	5
d. In directing cash flows to various managers	1	2	3	4	5

	Number of Years				
6. Our scope in judging investment returns appears to be	1–2	3	5	7	10 or more
7. Judgments of investment returns is best done over the following number of years	1–2	3	5	7	10 or more

8. Following are specific investment areas that, due to the nature of our business or other assets owned by us, we should emphasize or de-emphasize:

_____

_____

_____

_____

_____

[a]Or family situation.

"SCORING" YOUR QUESTIONNAIRE RESPONSES

Wide differences of opinion on any of the questions obviously demand attention—and resolution. The first three queries are more factual, while questions 4 through 8 are more qualitative. Divergent responses to questions 6 (your organization's or family's scope) and 7 ("proper" assessment period) represent a difference in viewpoint you can (and should) resolve immediately. Again, a *mixture* of responses—sharply varying answers, either by one influential person or by your group—suggests that you should discuss these issues more thoroughly.

Client Guide 1 should help you understand your investor self; it should create a realistic investment pace to be set by you and followed consistently by you and your manager. The probability should now be low that you will behave like Lewis Carroll's Tweedledee. You should now be exempt from the disruption and expense that result from considering yourself or your organization "brave" if in fact you will suffer from "a headache" as disappointing markets and other challenges present themselves. Instead, you have established the foundation for becoming a superior client and for forming a stronger team with your manager. This combination can only enhance your chances for superior results over the years.

A CLIENT/MANAGER "CHEMISTRY LESSON"

Being perceptive about your own investment personality is, of course, only part of the battle. Making sure a manager is *right for you* is another challenge—and a major goal of this book. You may not find, and you may not need, clones of your own personality. But neither do you want people with whom you will be uncomfortable. While it makes sense for some clients to balance risky income sources by making conservative investments, probabilities for long-term success are low if your managers represent the antithesis of your nature. That important role of money—to foster peace of mind—is likely to dissipate if the "investment chemistry" isn't right. As noted in Chapter 1, the manager who is superior for someone else may not be the manger who is superior for you!

Perhaps the best way to ensure maximum compatibility is to match your investment *personalities* with those of your (present or intended) manager. After all, somewhere there exists an investment manager Jack for every investment client Jill, so there is no reason why anyone should settle for incompatible or less-than-very-comfortable chemistry. You have to be careful not to make this judgment based on manager "attractiveness," good looks, impressive slide shows, entertainment potential—or, of course, past performance record alone.

This brings us to Client Guides 2 and 2a, which are nearly identical. Client Guide 2, "A Client Personality Questionnaire," should be completed by you before you entrust money to others; Client Guide 2a, "A Manager Personality Questionnaire," should be answered by any managers being evaluated by you. Manager responses—which are designed to delineate investing dispositions, styles, and tendencies—should mesh with your desires—and vice versa.

CLIENT GUIDE 2
A Client Personality Questionnaire

I (the client) believe I will be best served by a manager embracing the following characteristics:

1. Current income from our investments
   a. High current income is important to us
   b. Medium current income is required
   c. Current income is not of any consequence (We are "total return" investors)
2. Risk taking
   a. We can assume high risks
   b. We are medium-risk investors
   c. We have very low risk tolerance
3. Investment styles
   We are most comfortable with owning:
   a. Large-capitalization-company stocks only
   b. Medium-capitalization-company stocks only
   c. Small-capitalization-company stocks only
   d. A combination of companies of varying sizes, with manager having discretion as to the mix

4. Investment styles

   We are most comfortable with:

   a. Growth stocks

   b. Lower price/earnings (P/E) stocks

   c. Contrary-opinion securities (out-of-favor securities, which are likely to include struggling companies in more questionable industries or with more questionable competitive positions)

   d. Market timers

   e. A combination of styles

5. Desires/restrictions on use of cash in portfolio

   We are going to be happiest with managers taking:

   a. Extreme positions (cash possibly 50 to 100 percent of portfolio at any time)

   b. Active positions (cash possibly 25 to 50 percent of portfolio at any time)

   c. Moderate positions (cash at a maximum of 25 percent of portfolio at any time)

   d. Near fully invested positions (10 percent maximum cash at any time)

6. Investment objectives

   Our most important consideration is:

   a. To achieve exceptional performance

   b. To achieve above-average performance

   c. To achieve close-to-average or average performance

   Our specific goal in *exceptionally strong* markets is:

   d. Exceptional performance

   e. Above-average performance

   f. Average performance

   g. Below-average performance acceptable in "frothy" periods

   Our specific goal in "normal" markets is:

   h. Exceptional performance

   i. Above-average performance

   Our specific goal in very poor markets is:

   j. Exceptional performance

   k. Above-average performance

   l. Average performance

   m. Underperformance is acceptable here because we expect above-average or superior performance in very strong markets—and we know we cannot have it both ways!

Concerning volatility of the value of our portfolio, we:

    n.   Can stand up to several years of negative absolute returns

    o.   Can stand only 1 to 2 years of negative absolute returns

    p.   Can stand negative returns as long as the general market is negative, too

    q.   Cannot stand even a year of negative absolute returns

7. Preferable size of investment management firm
   a. Large firm
   b. Medium-size firm
   c. Small firm
   d. No opinion

8. Communications
   a. Written reports on a regular basis (i.e., quarterly)
   b. Telephone communication between written reports, if any, on about the following basis:

   _____

   c. _____ number of manager visits/year, of which _____ will be at our home base and _____ at the manager's home base.

9. Manager personality
   The best kind of individual to service us and manage the account is:
   a. Highly articulate
   b. Well educated
   c. Anybody, so long as he knows his business

10. Other special requests

   _____

   _____

   _____

   _____

Now here is the counterpart questionnaire to be completed by your manager or prospective manager.

CLIENT GUIDE 2a
A Manager Personality Questionnaire

The following best describes our investing style:

1. Current income from our investments
   a. High current income is emphasized by us
   b. Medium current income is our normal style
   c. Current income is not of any consequence (we are "total return" investors)

2. Risk taking
   a. We normally assume higher-risk investments
   b. We are medium-risk investors
   c. We have very low risk tolerance

3. Investment styles
   We are most comfortable with owning
   a. Large-capitalization-company stocks only
   b. Medium-capitalization-company stocks only
   c. Small-capitalization-company stocks only
   d. A combination of companies of varying sizes, with our having discretion as to the mix

4. Investment styles
   We are most comfortable with
   a. Growth stocks
   b. Lower P/E stocks
   c. Contrary-opinion securities (out-of-favor securities, which are likely to include struggling companies in more questionable industries or with more questionable competitive positions)
   d. Market timing
   e. A combination of styles

5. Our philosophy regarding the use of cash in portfolio
   Our philosophy is to take:
   a. Extreme positions (cash possibly 50 to 100 percent of portfolio at any time)
   b. Active positions (cash possibly 25 to 50 percent of portfolio at any time)
   c. Moderate positions (cash at a maximum of 25 percent of portfolio at any time)
   d. Near fully invested positions (10 percent maximum cash at any time)

6. Investment objectives
   Our most important consideration is:
   a. To achieve exceptional performance

b. To achieve above-average performance
c. To achieve close-to-average or average performance

Our specific goal in *exceptionally strong* markets is:
d. Exceptional performance
e. Above-average performance
f. Average performance
g. Below-average performance acceptable in "frothy" periods

Our specific goal in "normal" markets is:
h. Exceptional performance
i. Above-average performance

Our specific goal in very poor markets is:
j. Exceptional performance
k. Above-average performance
l. Average performance
m. Underperformance acceptable here because we expect above-average or superior performance in very strong markets— and we know we cannot have it both ways!

Concerning volatility of the value of our portfolios, we:
n. Do best with clients who can stand above-average volatility in exchange for above-average results.
o. Do best with clients who want no more than average volatility, realizing that somewhat above-average results are likely
p. Do best with clients whose assessment of returns is based on performance relative to the market (no absolute goals)
q. Do best with clients trying to avoid even a year of negative absolute returns

7. Our investment management firm is
   a. A large firm (_____ dollars under management; _____ number of accounts)
   b. A medium-size firm (_____ dollars under management; _____ number of accounts)
   c. A small firm (_____ dollars under management; _____ number of accounts)

8. Communications
   We submit to our clients:
   a. Written reports on a regular basis (i.e., quarterly)
   b. Telephone communication between written reports, if any, on about the following basis:

   _____

   c. We plan on _____ number of manager visits/year, of which _____ will be at your home base and _____ at our manager's home base.

Manager responses to items 1 through 8 of Client Guide 2a should be compared against your responses 1 through 8 on Client Guide 2. Obviously, the more similarities there are, the better the chance of the chemistry being right. Matching responses should be helpful to you in your manager selection and reassessment processes and in producing compatibilities that can only enhance investment success.

4

IMPROVING YOUR INVESTMENT RETURNS BY SETTING REALISTIC AND UNDERSTAND-ABLE GUIDELINES

He who holds the gold
makes the rules.

Ancient proverb

The acronym *GIGO*—which stands for *garbage in, garbage out*—is often used in computer circles, but it can be applied to many other aspects of life. If one provides inaccurate or inefficient inputs, one should expect similarly inaccurate or inefficient outputs.

There are many opportunities for GIGOs in client/manager relationships. One is the creation of vague or unreasonable guidelines. The truth is that considerable sums of money are frittered away because clients set—*and managers accept*—dicta that are destined to be violated.

Why do one or both parties engage in such destructive behavior? To begin with, many managers knowingly accept poorly defined or even ill-conceived client guidelines just as they accept fuzzy or unrealistic client demands. These managers rationalize their acceptance in many ways, some of which are: (1) they might be lucky enough to succeed for a while and collect some fees in the process; and (2) if they fail, the greatest loss is to the client, who the manager might contend deserves failure since he set unrealistic goals to begin with.

Clients might be excused for inconsistent or illogical demands on the grounds of investing naiveté. But that is a weak excuse; if you are to participate in the game, your responsibility is to learn the rules. *If you are to improve your returns, you absolutely must set practical investment objectives. Making this effort is at worst a "necessary evil" and at most a tool to create a consistent approach that should improve results over the years*. The article entitled "Rate Yourself as a Client," quoted in Chapter 1, summed this up well. The author, Anthony Jay, implored clients not to "try to teach your advisor his own job—[and] do not ask him to do yours. The distinction between ends and means is at the heart of your relationship. You are the expert on ends; he is the expert on means."

THE PURPOSES OF GOOD GUIDELINES AND OBJECTIVES

Whether you're an individual or institutional investor, there are four major reasons for producing well-considered, *written* guidelines. First, the effort usually helps you conclude what your realistic objectives should

Africa 961-968

Indians of North America 970

Canada 971

Central America 972

United States History — General 973
  Colonial 973.2
  American Revolution 973.3 & 973.4
  Civil War 973.6 & 973.7
  Modern 973.9

South America 980's

See also
  Archeology 913
  Foreign Affairs 327
  Political Science 320
  Immigrants 325
  Slavery & Emancipation 326
  Government 328-329
  U.S. Constitution 342
  Biography published before 1976   Biography Section

When you do not find a **specific** title on the shelf, it may be . . .

    1. already checked out
    2. in the new book display
    3. with returns not yet reshelved
    4. not checked-out but in use
    5. misshelved

959.7
959

Vietnam War
South East Asia

History Hunter's Browsing Guide
Dewey's Decimal Sequence

General World History	901-909
Ancient Civilizations (China, Egypt, Greece, Rome)	930-939
General European History	940
Middle Ages	940.1
Modern Europe	940.2
World War I	940.3 & 940.4
World War II	940.53 & 940.54
Great Britain	941 & 942
Germany & Eastern Europe	943
France	944
Italy	945
Spain & Portugal	946
Soviet Union	947
Scandinavia	948
Other European Countries	949
Asia — General	950
China	951
Japan & Korea	952
India	954
Middle East (Arabs & Israel)	956

be. It requires assessment of your financial, business, and personal investing characteristics—that is, a knowledge of your investor self. Second, well-stated objectives enhance your ability to judge your managers fairly; you can match risk taking and achievements against something reasonably definite. Third, good guidelines help your manager. Parameters are set and are there for confirmation at any time. And fourth, the effort improves communications between the two parties, both in the setting of the objectives and in later discussions of them.

CONSTRUCTING SOUND INVESTMENT OBJECTIVES

It is crucial to prepare properly for the drafting of what is to be your "investment constitution." Start out with the right attitudes; that is, do not confuse objective setting with rigidity. All guidelines must be dynamic; they must be open to change (but not indiscriminate change). *Soundly conceived guidelines certainly should not be altered as often as markets change.* Your circumstances can, of course, change, and portfolios must change with them, but *you must not confuse the natural urge to join in the market's ups and run from the downs with changes in your circumstances!*

As in all good general constitutions, you should also define the separate responsibilities of any people involved in your investment decision making. This includes any client representative(s) directly responsible, the bodies to whom he reports, and the investment managers. You cannot expect the best results unless these individuals are all well informed about their roles.

Now you are ready for goal-setting specifics, the first of which is to separate your primary from your secondary objectives. To do this, you should clarify: (1) to whom the money belongs; (2) what its intended purpose is; and (3) what the resulting investment time frame is. Answering these questions will allow you then to focus on defining the level of risk that may be assumed. *Which comes first, making money or avoiding loss?* And to what degree? As indicated in Chapter 3, it is normal to desire a lot

of the former and a little of the latter, but that is not a realistic expectation. Agreeing on ownership, purpose, time frame, and risk can be
arduous, but working toward an agreement is a necessity. The clearer the
definition, the greater the opportunity for investment success—financial
rewards and peace of mind.

Obviously, this process is important for both individuals and institutions. If the funds are personal and intended, for example, to make a
down payment on a home or to provide for your retirement years, these
considerations (ownership, purpose, time frame, and risk) are reasonably
clear. So they would be if the money belonged to "Junior" and its purpose
were to provide for his college education. Other personal goals may be
less clear but definitely worth the probing efforts.

Institutional goals are often more complicated. Groups overseeing
jointly trusteed labor/management funds, for example, often have to
grapple with the ownership issue. The labor side may insist that the funds
are ultimately theirs and that they should have maximum control,
whereas management may contend that pension payments are their
responsibility and therefore theirs to dictate.

The question of making money or avoiding loss can also become deeply
philosophical. In the business world, a savings plan, even with corporate
matching contributions, is the employees' money; as such, it demands a
different investment mind-set from pension payments, which amount to
a corporate guarantee. Even within the latter, there are gray areas. For
example, most people consider defined benefits (specific dollar pension
payments) as static, but an organization might someday decide to compensate for an erosion of recipient purchasing power brought about by
extraordinary inflation. Moreover, the area of undefined benefits (where
the contributions are defined but where the benefits can vary sharply
depending on investment results) poses additional complications. Unless
the contributor allows a recipient to choose his investment vehicles and
meld these with his personal risk posture, the contributor is making
judgments for sharply differing objectives. Some contributor clients are
willing to "bet the store" (some actually earn more on their pension
portfolios than they do on the company's operating assets) without adequate consideration for those whose money is involved or its true in-

tended purpose. Other contributors forgo considerable upside potential in exchange for less volatility and more protection against the downside.

Like the broken record, I repeat: In setting objectives, it is crucial to define whose funds are involved, the purpose intended for them, and the time allotted to achieve that purpose—and which comes first, making money or avoiding loss, and to what degree?

SETTING REAL (ADJUSTED FOR INFLATION) RETURN GOALS

Clients have suffered understandable frustration in choosing proper investment goals. There are many stock and bond indices that can be used for comparison, none of which is sacrosanct. Likewise, absolute returns have been volatile, and these have been accompanied by volatile inflation experience. As a result, more and more clients have shifted to goals adjusted for inflation.

Since preserving purchasing power is a very crucial objective of most investors, the quest for *real* (i.e., *after* inflation) returns is a logical one. The trouble is that such goals are almost certain to be unrealistic in high inflation periods. Bond markets are likely to be negatively affected during such times. Stock markets may do well for a while, but the adverse effects of lower P/E multiples (prompted by competing high interest rates) and subsequent earnings declines (if monetary authorities attempt to halt the inflationary spiral) make for eventual difficulties here, too. Thus, the "double whammy" of high inflation and loss of principal produces a very deep "hole" from which very dramatic recovery becomes necessary if the goal is to be achieved. A good (but frustrating) example of this occurred in 1973 and 1974, when cumulative negative absolute returns from stocks amounted to approximately 36 percent compounded, while the inflation rate amounted to just under 20 percent. So the experience of an investor who simply matched the market was a negative compound real return of approximately 56 percent. Clients might have had managers whose stock returns were better than the market's −36 percent for those 2 years, but even the exceptional ones who were down only half the average market decline (i.e., down only 18 percent) still had −38 percent real returns to make up. The dramatic 1975 and 1976 market recoveries of around +68 percent produced a real offset of 54 percent, since inflation in those years ran 14 percent. Remember, however, that the 54 percent real recovery from the 56 percent decline did *not* rebuild the portfolio to within 2 percent of its original value. Just as capital reduced by half must subsequently double to reach the break-even point, the market-matching investor of 1973 and 1974 required a 127 percent advance to break even (the 56 percent decline left only 44 percent of buying power, which had to increase 1.27 times to reach its original amount). The moral of the story is obvious: Sizable declines require more sizable recoveries to achieve success; and high inflation periods present special problems. In short, you will probably have to adopt long-term views of real return goals in times of high inflation.

THE IMPORTANCE OF WRITTEN GUIDELINES

Many people fear that we may someday be literally buried in paper. Despite this, putting thoughts on the old papyrus has its advantages. Writing out ideas is a good discipline; the effort forces more concentration, just as it creates a paper trail that allows for consistent comparison and later communication.

The following is an outline of the steps you should take in the construction of good guidelines, including the "right language" designed to avoid subsequent misunderstandings.

A MANUAL FOR CONSTRUCTING GOOD GUIDELINES

Clarify Your Financial Position

Describe your or your organization's financial position, summarizing your balance sheet and income prospects, including the potential variability of your circumstances or business. If your position is liable to be volatile or cyclical, indicate this, along with the conditions most likely to cause the greatest disturbances. Are you, for example, a beneficiary or victim of inflation? Are you vulnerable to foreign competition and/or a strong U.S. dollar? Summarize your financial character through Client Guide 1.

Describe Your Investment Attitudes

1.   State your willingness to condone portfolio volatility and/or risk. Complete Client Guide 2 depicting the pattern of results you prefer over time. Anything that serves to clarify your risk posture and your tolerance for pain is integral to a good statement of objectives. Thus, if avoiding large risks is paramount, state this *along with your understanding that gains are bound to be tempered in the process.* If you can tolerate volatility, reassure your manager that you recognize investing to be a two-way street and that you are prepared to be patient through difficult periods.

If you have a maximum tolerance for percentage declines in any given period, say so; for example, "A loss of _____ percent in any _____-month span exceeds our loss threshold." Ensure that your estimates are not visceral ones that are inconsistent with either your objectives or the practical facts of investment life. A limitation of 10 to 20 percent losses in a year sounds reasonable, but you may be forcing an equity manager to retain substantial cash in your portfolio, thereby exposing you to the inherent conditions of extreme market timing. Hence, you should state your attitude on cash usage. If you expect market timing, say so; but indicate that you are familiar with the possibilities for nonparticipation in big upside movements. If compiling cash creates problems for your desired total asset mix, set the limits of its use.

2.   Quality requirements should be stressed, although these can be as difficult to define as risk tolerance. If you wish to limit your manager's actions in any way, *you've got to say so.* Those limitations might include: ownership of smaller companies; balance sheet or income requirements of companies owned; quality standards set by rating agencies; holdings of

unlisted stocks, foreign securities, private placements, options, and so on. Preclusions should be made with care, however; make sure there are good reasons for them, and see that they are not unduly hindering your manager(s).

3.   Communicate any maximum-size holdings by security or type; for example, "Ownership of any stock limited to _____ percent of portfolio at cost and _____ percent at market." Or, to shield you against market-ability problems: "Manager's total holdings (among all accounts) may not exceed _____ percent of average trading volume over the past 6 months." (Careful here—volume figures change with the market in general and with stock popularity.)

4.   Isolate and identify your own "hangups." These might range from exclusion of certain industry groups or individual stocks to portfolio turnover maximums, numbers of securities owned (some definition of too few or too many), or policies on gains and losses.

5.   Prescribe minimum income requirements, if any.

6.   State clearly the amount of discretion you have delegated to your manager. Is he responsible for only a portion of your assets? If so, is he to be guided at all by investment policies followed elsewhere? Where does he have a free hand and where not?

Client Guide 3: A Model Set of Objectives

The following guidelines should serve as a format for any client to follow. The Client Guide 3 has been modeled for a conservative pension-type account, but minor changes will make it useful for individuals or for other institutional clients. It has been simulated for a mythical client with a number of managers separately hired for fixed-income, equities, and balanced (both bond and stock) portfolios. Any of these characteristics may differ from yours, but two things should not: the clarity and specificity of the investment objectives.

CLIENT GUIDE 3
A Model Set of Investment Objectives

I. *Our Company*

Our company is one with a strong and liquid balance sheet and reasonably good net income prospects. We do not consider our business to be particularly sensitive to normal business cycles. We would certainly not be exempt from a serious economic slowdown (i.e., depression), however, and thus we have a normal need for protection against such an environment. We consider our business to have above-average protection against moderate to high inflation (up to approximately 10 percent), but we are uncertain how much protection we would possess against very high (double-digit) cost-of-living rises. It is *our* responsibility to balance equity-type (common stock and real estate) investments with sufficient (and high-enough-quality) fixed-income investments to allow us to make our regular contributions to our fund for up to 5 or so years of the worst of any economic scenarios.

We look, therefore, to fixed-income investments for reasonably high current income and for a hedge against serious deflation; we look to common stocks for protection against moderate inflationary conditions, as well as for participation in normal economic times; and we look to real estate investments for protection against high inflationary periods, as well as for participation in more normal times.

II. *Our Account*

This account is tax exempt. Realized gains and losses do not entail payment of taxes, but excessive realization of either can affect required contributions on our part to the fund. The account represents our only pension plan. It covers all salaried and hourly wage employees. Benefits have been defined; contributions are variable and are based on actuarial and other assumptions, as well as on investment results. *The plan is the guarantee of pension benefits of our company to all officers and employees.* Our contributions have been based on assumptions of annual salary increases of 7 percent, on investment returns averaging 9 percent (which, to provide a margin of error, is 2.5 percent below our expectations), and on inflation assumptions of 6 percent.

III. *Our Pension Plan Committee and Our Assessment of Investment Results.*

We have assessed our committee's internal investment tendencies. We expect to abide by the goals that follow, exercising reasonable patience. We do not expect to be reactive to short-term investment developments, recognizing that a complete market cycle must be considered before concluding quantitatively on managerial capabilities. We consider a 3- to 5-year period to be normal for such assessment, but we anticipate making interim qualitative judgments and expect our managers to cooperate in supplying information on their internal personnel changes, on any changes in their ownership, or on any factors potentially affecting efficient carrying out of their duties.

IV.   *Our Goals and Related Instructions.*

Although our company is sound financially and relatively noncyclical in nature, we do not choose to take significant risks with our pension plan. Our quality standards are indicated below. These are to be supplemented by other fundamental risk assessments that we expect to mirror our "low to medium-risk" posture. These risk assessments will be supplemented by a maximum beta portfolio measurement of 1.10,[a] and we expect to monitor the fundamental qualities (earnings, financial position, etc.) of our portfolios.

To paraphrase our risk posture, we are more concerned about minimizing losses than about maximizing gains; we would prefer to overperform on a relative basis during negative-return periods, underperform on a relative basis during ebullient periods (where general markets are up sharply or where participation in lower-grade or excessively valued individual securities dominate), and achieve above-average but not dynamic positives during normal markets.

Our only income requirement is for common stock yields to be no less than 33 percent of the yield of the S&P 500 Stock Index.

Quality requirements: On average (weighted for dollars invested), not below "A-" S&P ratings for both bonds and stocks.

Cash holdings by managers: Cash (defined as investments with maturities under 1 year) to be held to a maximum of 20 percent of a manager's designated portfolio. Manager may request an increase in this 20 percent limitation through communication with our committee. (The present 20 percent maximum has been set to retain a certain overall portfolio structure for our account.)

As mentioned, our investment assumptions for accounting purposes are 9 percent annualized returns. These goals have been conservatively set. Our manager goal is to achieve approximately an 11.5 percent annualized total return over the next 5 to 10 years, taking into account current yields from bonds, stocks, and real estate and using reasonably conservative assumptions for capital appreciation prospects. The following are the derivations of our total return goals (assuming a 5- to 10-year holding period):

[a]Chapters 6 and 9 cover Beta measurement.

Fixed income	10%	
Common stocks	12%	
Real estate	12%	

We encourage communication from our managers as to the reasonableness of these projected returns, particularly if they are deemed to be unrealistically high.

We have set our portfolio structure/diversification plans as follows:

Manager Responsibility	Percentage Allotment (of Our Portfolio)[b]	Percentage Allotment to Fixed Income	Percentage Allotment to Equities
Fixed income only	20	20	0
Common stocks only	30	0	30
Balanced portfolio: with portions assigned to:	40		
Fixed income (minimum 30% of balance)		12	0
Common stocks (maximum 70% of balance)		0	28
Real estate	10	0	10
Totals	100	32	68

This portfolio balance, along with anticipated investment returns from each asset, produces our goal of 11.5 percent total return, as follows:

Asset	Percentage of Our Portfolio Return	Percentage of Our Approximate Annual Total Return from the Asset	Percentage of Our Approximate Annual Total Return to Our Total Portfolio
Fixed income	32	10	3.2
Common stocks	58	12	7.0
Real estate	10	12	1.2
Total	100	—	11.4

[b]At market prices.

Balanced Portfolio Managers. As indicated, balanced portfolio managers can have up to 70 percent of their account in equities (common stocks). They can alter the mix of their portfolio, however, and can reduce such equity exposure, but only down to 50 percent of their designated monies under management. Thus, fixed income will constitute a minimum of 30 percent of portfolio, up to a maximum of 50 percent.

Reporting to us must be clear. Balanced managers must carry two distinct portions of our assets—one for equity exposure and one for fixed income. Any cash set aside should be designated as part of each of the two, so that we can assess your degree of conviction about each asset, determine whether you are following our 20 percent maximum cash policy, and assess performance most efficiently.

Performance Goals and Reporting: While absolute performance attainment is our primary goal, our investment committee will utilize relative performance as an additional criterion for manager assessment. Comparisons against the S&P 500 and/or an index that closely reflects a manager's style will be utilized for equities; a combined Shearson/Lehman and Salomon Brothers index will be used for fixed; and a weighted composite of the equity and fixed-income indices will be used for the balanced portfolio, along with performance comparisons of managers investing with like objectives, if such can be reasonably established. Real estate will be compared with property performance indices to be determined.

We recognize the difficulty of our managers (possibly excluding real estate) achieving any of our goals under conditions of very high inflation (over 10 percent for extended periods).

Our committee has considered all aspects of our lower-risk philosophies—our willingness to trade off large gain potentials in favor of more moderate expectations. We are hopeful that our returns will be somewhat more predictable and consistent, and that our fund will rank in the top quartile of pension funds during declining markets, while probably ranking above the median during rising markets and below the median during very ebullient ones.

V. *Restrictions*

Managers will have full discretion over portfolio investment decisions but will conform to our guidelines, with the following specific restrictions. If managers at any time consider such restrictions burdensome to their management or injurious to our potential investment returns (our risk posture considered), we encourage your immediate communication to us.

52

Equities

Maximum cash positions of 20 percent of equity portfolio

Maximum of 10 percent position of stocks denominated in foreign currencies

No private placements, venture capital, or other securities not pubicly traded

No ownership of options or futures contracts without prior approval of committee

No borrowing on the part of our account

Without prior approval of committee, no ownership of any single security over 7 percent (at market valuation) of portfolio, or any industry group over 20 percent of portfolio

No holdings of companies engaged in our business, described broadly as "wholesale and retail food chains." (Note: equity performance indices used for comparative purposes will be adjusted for results from such "wholesale and retail food chains," if these holdings at any time have significant impact on such comparisons)

Minimum quality of equity holdings (dollar weighted): S&P "A−" rating

Maximum holdings of common stocks with market capitalization values below $500 million: 25 percent of any manager's portfolio

Fixed Income

Average quality of bond portfolio no less than S&P "A−" rating

Without prior approval of committee, maximum maturity of bond holdings (dollar weighted) to be 12 years

Spelling Out Communication Requirements

Although the obligations for client/manager communications are seldom included in written guidelines, there is no reason why they should not be. After all, the responsibilities should be dictated by you.

Your attitude toward interim written and telephone contact by the manager should be clear. What is expected, and by whom, should not be left vague. For example, you should probably require consistent communications of the following: important changes recommended by your manager in asset mix and portfolio structure, plus notification of unusual events affecting market value of assets. In addition, significant internal changes in your manager organization should be reported posthaste to your direct contact.

Personal meetings and other communications directed by you should be as regular as possible. It is as important to see or talk to the manager who is doing well as it is to communicate with the one who is faltering. Just as you should not judge a person's appearance only after lengthy cosmetic preparation or only as he or she crawls out of bed in the morning, do not wait for extremes in performance to praise *or* damn your managers. Try to see them at all stages—you will get to know their strengths and weaknesses and their idiosyncrasies better this way.

Conclusions

You have a responsibility to be practical and specific in your demands from managers. Expectations and limitations, however, should be similar in the minds of both parties. Neither of you should be able to complain before, during, or after the management of the account about inconsistencies or unrealistic requirements. No "I demand the maximum upside, but I don't want much risk" or "I expect to be heavy in stocks while they're rising but out of them when they're falling" expectations should exist. A better client/manager relationship starts with the preparation of well-defined, mutually accepted, and well-documented plans. The natural fallout from this should be (definitely) fewer surprises and (probably) improved investment results.

5

INVESTMENT CYCLES AND STYLES: HOW UNDERSTANDING THEM CAN HELP YOU DIFFERENTIATE LUCK FROM SKILL AND MAKE YOU A MORE ASTUTE INVESTOR

You don't have to be an investment expert to be a successful client, but you certainly should know some basics about investing profitably. There are two fundamentals that you absolutely must understand: (1) that cycles and styles dominate markets and are as responsible as anything else for producing good or bad returns; and (2) that the investing process, including consideration of these cycles and styles, can be *very* inexact. No matter what you have been led to believe, there is often a thin line between making solid decisions and having circumstances beyond your control influence the outcome.

Am I hinting that luck can play a big part in investing through others?

The answer is a decided *Yes*—which means that you must learn to determine how much luck and how much solid decision making are affecting your results.

Let's talk then about cycles, styles, and luck.

If conditions were static, these three considerations would be less important. Investors would quickly recognize the most and least attractive companies and, up to some price limitation, they would direct their dollars mainly toward the most promising and away from the least promising participants. The trouble is that conditions are never static. Economies change in direction and character; demands are variable; the supply of goods is constantly changing; costs jump up and down for a variety of reasons, as do pricing levels and profits for different industries and companies; and people place varying values on investment vehicles for both sound and unsound reasons.

These inevitable fluctuations create the greatest problems but also the greatest challenges and opportunities for you, either as an individual investor or as an investing client. The problem portion may seem confusing if you are a client. After all, you might assume that managers can handle these variables. Isn't that what they are paid handsomely to do? Isn't it their job to anticipate cycles and styles and profit from them?

That is their job, but they are hindered in their mission for two major reasons. First, few managers have the interest, conviction, or flexibility to cover all the bases necessary to prosper in all types of environments. It is difficult to be all things to all people in life, and it is equally tough to be a successful investor under the many different conditions certain to be faced over time. Most managers, therefore, develop styles—investment philosophies with which they are most comfortable and most effective. Specialties are condoned—actually, sought—in other fields, so it is only natural that this should be the case in investment management.

Second, the very inexact investor valuations of securities complicate the lives of both managers and clients. You may be presented with valuation models from managers that hint of exactness, but investing precludes precision—mainly because prices result from what investors *expect from the future*. Price earnings multiple, dividend yield, and book value projections that rely on past history may provide clues to future events, but these can be very imprecise clues. Even with identical assumptions, valuations are at best ballpark guesstimates. The most astute investors could argue interminably but never reach a conclusion over valuations that would cause 20 percent, or 30 percent, or even greater differences in the market price of any security. In the end, the actual difference may result from errors in judgment by others!

A perfect illustration of investment inexactness (which is bound to affect you and your manager) is the unpredictable success that I personally experienced in the 1960s and early 1970s.

When I entered the investment business in 1955, stocks were still sought by countless investors more for income than for capital appreciation (as indicated in Chapter 2). Premiums were paid for certain companies that appeared to have more attractive futures, but limits generally existed if dividend yields were particularly low. Fortunately, I saw flaws in the emphasis placed on current yields; it didn't require any genius to calculate how much more favorable it could be to buy into companies that were slated to hike their dividends substantially over the years than to buy high current yields that seemed destined to remain static or decline. Dividend returns weren't everything, however. It was equally sensible to project what higher future reported profits could do for stock price enhancement as opposed to investment in companies essentially going nowhere.

What occurred was beyond my fondest dreams and those of even the most devoted growth stock proponents. There were interruptions, but the basic trend from the mid-1950s through 1972 was one of favorable economic conditions that allowed for both growth in earnings and improved investor psychology; currency levels that stimulated foreign expansion and profitability by U.S. companies; and, most important, a greater and greater desire on the part of the investors, particularly institutions, to increase their holdings in these very growth-oriented securities.

You would probably be impressed if I could state that I was able to foresee all these development taking place. But I did not, nor do I imagine that *anyone* did, at least to the extent that the conditions emerged. A candid appraisal would be that *everyone* was presented with a gift.

Some of the success was richly deserved. Many managers had shown foresight, confidence, sensitivity to investor perceptions, and other sound traits. But who could *or should* have justified the valuations eventually accorded? The same people who had well-reasoned mathematical (or intuitive) models that suggested that prices of certain stocks deserved 15 times earnings versus an original level of 8, 10, or 12 were soon finding ways to support 20 times earnings and more. This trend was magnified in the late 1960s and early 1970s as multiples jumped to 25, 30, 40, and higher P/E's. Investors rationalized purchases of certain growth stocks almost regardless of market price. "It isn't the price that counts, it's the company," the staunchest advocates insisted.

The disaster that ensued (growth stocks collapsed and remained depressed for the next 4 years*) illustrates the severe overenthusiasm and overvaluation that had developed. Most growth stock investors, then, had (earlier) received what is crudely known today as a "no brainer" gift.

There is another side to style manias, such as this growth stock experience. While it is possible that one segment of the market is paralleled by all other styles, this is not generally the case. One investor's bonanza is often another's downfall, as money is shifted from one type of security to another. *Hence, the disparities in results from one managerial concentration or style to another is likely to be very large.* And, to repeat, possibly for flimsy reasons!

You can see then why it is imperative to understand that the movement

---

*Many for much longer.

of securities from "fair evaluation" to excessive evaluation (and vice versa) can become heavily influenced by luck.

The implications of this fact are:

1. Market moves in which luck plays a larger and larger part make it harder and harder for you to be a perceptive client. Extra effort on your part should be made to:

    a. Recognize managers who may be recipients of "gifts." Be careful not to equate exceptional performance with wisdom likely to persist.

    b. Exercise empathy for any negative events that are beyond reasonable control of managers. Understand how those whose styles are "out" may be victims of others' foolishness. Probe also whether the very managers who foresaw favorable trends early have suffered the misfortune of selling just before excessive valuations occurred (thereby underperforming).

2. Risk assessment is confusing during under- and overvaluation periods, particularly if the most inefficiently priced securities are those possessing fine basic qualities (such as the growth stock illustration).

It *will* be difficult to separate bad luck from extremely good fortune, but it will be worth the effort!

RECOGNIZING CYCLES AND STYLES AND THEIR EFFECT ON PERFORMANCE

You will be a more productive client if you expect style changes, ascertain what effects these trends are having on performance, recognize manager style differences, and constantly relate performance results to these managerial characteristics.

While not all markets lend themselves to neat style assessment, most decidedly do. Not all managers fit into neat styles, either, but again, many do. Consultants can help with differentiation here, but there are caveats for you to consider. In some cases, consultants' categorizing of styles is a "forced package" intended to glorify their services. In other cases, their categorization lacks adequate backup. In most cases, they provide a worthwhile background (but one that probably requires interpretation and questioning).

Despite these cautions, you should learn to be very sensitive to cycles and styles within the economy, and particularly within investment markets and investment manager organizations. Client Guide 4 should heighten your awareness of these factors.

The information in Client Guide 4 can be supplied to you by either a manager or a consultant. Column (1) is an extension of Chapter 3's Manager Questionnaire (Client Guide 2a). The column provides more specific, quantified information on how a manager is likely to structure a portfolio of stocks, divided:

1. By size of companies normally owned
2. By "company type" (high growth vs. slow; cyclical vs. noncyclical; high book value vs. low, etc.)
3. By high, average, or low current yield
4. By high, average, or low price/earnings multiple
5. By the extent of cash and market timing normally utilized
6. By the average volatility of market price to be expected

Column (2) compares the above considerations to the market (the S&P 500). Your knowing where a manager normally differs from the market provides a good frame of reference for you—a clear picture of his style. And column (3) shows how well or poorly these same investment categories performed over the past several years. To simplify your analysis, the plus and minus performance numbers of the various groupings of column (3) have been summarized on a 1-to-5 scale, with 5 indicating the best relative performance and 1 the worst. Your noting the responses to the Guide will inform you better of manager styles and investment markets and allow you to match the two. Do not expect precision, but at least you can now spot those managers whose styles have been carried by waves of euphoria or depression by investors. Like other Guides, it focuses attention on high-priority considerations, just as it leads you to efficient inquiries.

CLIENT GUIDE 4

Statement of Manager Investment Style and Risk Taking

	(1) Percent of Manager's Equity Portfolio Expected to be in:		(2) Approximate Percentage of S&P 500 Represented by These Categories	(3) The Market Performance Results for the Various Groupings over the:				
	Range	Normal Target		Latest Year	Year Before	Latest −2	Latest −3	Latest −4
I. *Size of companies owned (defined as market capitalization of companies):*								
Large capitalization (over $4 billion)	30–50	45	7	5	4	5	4	—
Medium capitalization ($1.5–4 billion)	30–50	35	33	4	2	4	5	—
Small-to-medium capitalization ($0.5–1.5 billion)	5–15	10	33	3	3	2	3	—
Small capitalization ($0.1–0.5 billion)	5–10	8	15	2	1	3	2	—
Tiny capitalization (under $0.1 billion)	0–5	2	2	1[a]	5[a]	1[a]	1[a]	—
		100	100					

	(1) Percent of Manager's Equity Portfolio Expected to be in:		(2) Approximate Percentage of S&P 500 Represented by These Categories	(3) The Market Performance Results for the Various Groupings over the:				
	Range	Normal Target		Latest Year	Year Before	Latest −2	Latest −3	Latest −4
II. *Type* of companies owned:								
A. Normally noncyclical growth over 3–5 years								
High growth (>20%/year)	0–10	5	2	1[a]	1	3	5	—
Strong growth (15–20%/year)	5–15	8	5	2[a]	2	2	4	—
Medium growth (10–15%/year)	8–20	10	15	3	4	1	3	—
Defensive/slower growth (5–9%/year)	4–12	5	20	4	3	5	2	—
Very slow growth (1–4%/year)	0–5	2	3	5	5	4	1	—
Total noncyclical growth		30	45					
B. Cyclical growth								
High growth (>20%/year)	0–10	3	1	1	1	3	5	—
Strong growth (15–20%/year)	5–15	12	7	2	2	2	4	—

Medium growth (10–15%/year)	10–25	13	10	4	3	5	2	—
Defensive/slower growth (5–9%/year)	5–15	10	11	3	4	4	3	—
Very slow growth (1–4%/year)	0–5	2	6	5	5	1	1	—
Total cyclical growth		40	35					
C. Cyclicals	10–30	20	15	1[a]	4	5	2	—
D. High asset (book value)	0–15	10	5	5	5	2	1	—
Total		100	100					
III. Current (dividend) yield:								
Very high income (>7%)	0–10	3	9	5	5	3	1	—
High income (5–7%)	5–20	10	12	4	2	1	1	—
Medium income (3–5%)	40–70	62	33	1	2	4	4	—
Low income (1–3%)	10–30	20	30	2	3	5	4	—
No current yield	0–10	5	16	3	4	3	3	—
Total		100	130					
IV. Normal portfolio price earnings multiple (relative to the S&P 500)								
60–80%				3	5	4	1	—
81–90%				4	5	4	1	—
91–100%				5	4	3	3	—

X (=100%)

| | (1) Percent of Manager's Equity Portfolio Expected to be in: | | (2) Approximate Percentage of S&P 500 Represented by These Categories | (3) The Market Performance Results for the Various Groupings over the: | | | | |
	Range	Normal Target		Latest Year	Year Before	Latest −2	Latest −3	Latest −4
101–110%		X		4	3	5	2	—
111–120%				3	2	2	4	—
121–140%				2	1	1	5	—
141–160%				1	1	1	5	—
Above 160%				1	1	1	5	—
V. *Market timing* (maximum cash positions)								
Tiny (5%)	0–10	5	N.A.	N.A.	N.A.	N.A.	N.A.	N.A.
Very small (6–10%)	10–20	15	N.A.	N.A.	N.A.	N.A.	N.A.	N.A.
Moderate (11–20%)	40–60	50	N.A.	N.A.	N.A.	N.A.	N.A.	N.A.
Medium (21–30%)	20–40	30	N.A.	N.A.	N.A.	N.A.	N.A.	N.A.
Large (31–50%)	0	0	N.A.	N.A.	N.A.	N.A.	N.A.	N.A.
Very large (50–100%)	0	0	N.A.	N.A.	N.A.	N.A.	N.A.	N.A.

VI. Market Volatility[a]
(beta of portfolios excluding cash)

Very low (below 0.80)	0–10	5	5	5	5	4	—
Low (0.81–0.95)	10–30	25	13	5	1	3	5	3	—
Low/moderate (0.96–1.00)	10–30	25	16	3	2	4	1[a]	—
Moderate (1.01–1.10)	10–20	15	39	3	4	3	3	—
Moderate/high (1.11–1.25)	10–20	15	13	3	4	1	2	—
High (1.26–1.50)	5–15	10	6	2	4	2	1[a]	—
Very high (above 1.50)	0–10	5	8	1[a]	3	4	3	—
		100	100					

[a]Very extreme increases/decreases relative to the market.

The Guide is best used in four ways: (1) to remind you what has occurred in the markets over the time you are assessing, with particular emphasis on how styles may have affected performance; (2) to allow you to assess how much of a manager's success or failure may have been due to accentuated style movements; (3) to force managers to state their styles as accurately as possible and in similar terms; and (4) to enable you to judge whether managers have been in fact following their stated philosophies.

Stock market results over the past 17 years only emphasize the importance of these realizations:

1969. Star performers were small- to medium-capitalization "growth stocks." Exceptional results came from managers who benefited from a new-issue (i.e., companies coming public for the first time) craze.

1970. General market was down, but the worst experience came from the very stars of 1968 and 1969—as the new-issue craze and the overvaluation of small companies created sharp declines.

1971–1972. Emergence of the so-called Nifty Fifty large-capitalization growth stock mania. Managers with big positions in these stocks were practically the only outstanding performers.

1973–1974. Two years of sharp general market declines. But the worst-looking managers were the very ones who prospered from 1968 to 1972, as the big and small growth stocks now fell precipitously from their prior lofty levels. The best performing managers of 1973 and 1974 were those who raised considerable cash, as this was by far the best performing asset. Hence, the more popular managers became the "market timers."

1975–1976. Sudden and significant rebound occurred in the stock market. The vast majority of timers were caught with too much cash; their performance went from the top of the heap in 1974 to the bottom in 1975. Growth stock managers continued to underperform, as emphasis now shifted to cyclical stock enthusiasts. The latter, benefiting from investor enthusiasm for what was forecast as a new era of "pricing power" for industries such as aluminum, chemicals, copper, and steel, suddenly became the star performers and money shifted in this direction.

1977–1978.   Pricing power became but a temporary aberration; cyclical stocks began underperforming. The same managers who had the best numbers in the prior 2 years fell toward the bottom. The market showed little follow-through, and the best strategy became one of fast rotation among industry groups. The most popular managers became the "group rotaters."

1979–1980.   Group rotation became less productive. Three industry groups dominated the market: energy, defense/aerospace, and technology—with reemergence of enthusiasm for smaller growth stocks in these three industries and others. Client money shifted to those who stayed with these groups and added to them.

1981–1982.   Energy and high-tech stocks collapsed, the former for the full 2 years and the latter till mid-1982—after which a sharp rally occurred (in high-tech). Top-performing managers were those with little or no energy exposure, as this group went from over 30 percent of the S&P 500 to around 14 percent. Growth stocks began performing better.

1983.   Small-cap stocks and new issues went through a craze similar to that of 1969. Money flowed quickly to managers with this style, as results had been dramatic since mid-1982. Soon thereafter, the small-cap, and particularly high-tech, stocks collapsed. The best performers became those who suffered through the late 1970s and early 1980s with cyclicals (or those who anticipated change and invested in "washed-out" industries). The big winners, however, were the high asset value (understated book value) plays that attracted cash tender offers, buyouts, and so on. Large-cap growth stocks fared poorly.

1984–1985.   Buyout candidates became the stars. Growth stocks suffered through mid-1985, partly due to the U.S. dollar's skyrocketing (which reversed itself as the year progressed). Small-cap stocks, particularly high-tech, were decimated.

You can see that it would have taken one very flexible—and very fortunate—manager to shift profitably through the full spectrum of changes that occurred over these 17 years. Some of the better-performing managers shifted strategies profitably several times along the way, but it would have required great precision and good fortune to rotate enough to be a top performer year by year or to produce maximum gains. The corollary is that most managers should have been expected to have both "hot" and "cold" periods. The following (very approximate) summary emphasizes this. (Note: Groups shown all in uppercase letters were new entries into either the most profitable or least profitable categories; the groups that then remained in their new category are shown in lowercase letters.)

The investment lesson is obvious and basic: Conditions change constantly; and what goes up is likely to come down (often soon). The client lesson is equally obvious: *Money moved to those who have the best recent records is likely to mean buying just before a fall*. In addition, patterns suggest that clients need patience with even the better managers, since they, too, will suffer from occasional erratic performance.

Later chapters will prepare you to take specific advantage of conditions like these. For the moment, accept the fact that *you should school yourself to avoid the trap of following what has "worked" most recently*.

Client Guide 5 (shown in Figure 5.1) should help you accomplish just this. *The Guide provides a practical look at how industry cycles and investment styles tend to rotate, and how investors generally, and investment management clients in particular, normally react to these cycles and styles*.

The Guide is called "The Endless Circle of Clients Zigging While Cycles Are Zagging" because that is exactly what normally happens.

Follow the top portion of the figure first, starting with 1, then moving on to 2, 3, and 4. Then read the explanations *inside* the circle (1.a through 4.a), reminding yourself that this is how clients normally respond to the cycles and styles of the *outside* portions of the circle.

It is important to repeat that, *unfortunately, investment results and client actions are NOT synchronized for future success*. If you read 1, and 1.a in that order, then 2 and 2.a, and so on, you will see how disjointed they are. To achieve the most productive buying and selling requires a distinct shift in attitude and in cash flow directions. For example, the most favorable *investment* points are obviously the outside circle positions of 4 and 1—just when client inclinations 4.a and 1.a are most negative. The least favorable point is late 2—exactly when you (2.a) are

Years	Most Profitable Areas	Least Profitable
1969	SMALLER GROWTH COMPANIES	
1970		SMALLER GROWTH
1971	LARGE-CAP GROWTH COMPANIES	CYCLICAL STOCKS
		SLOW GROWTH STOCKS
1972	large-cap growth	smaller growth
		slow growth
		cyclical stocks
1973	large-cap growth*	
	MARKET TIMERS	
	SLOW GROWTH	
1974	market timers	LARGE-CAP GROWTH
	slow growth	
1975	CYCLICALS	MARKET TIMERS
		SLOW GROWTH
		large-cap growth
1976	cyclicals	large-cap growth
		market timers
1977	GROUP ROTATORS	CYCLICALS
	GROWTH STOCKS	
1978	group rotators	cyclicals
	growth stocks	
1979	ENERGY	GROWTH STOCKS
		group rotators
		growth stocks
1980	energy	
	TECHNOLOGY	
1981	GROWTH STOCKS	ENERGY
		TECHNOLOGY
1982	TECHNOLOGY*	energy
	SMALL-CAP COMPANIES	TECHNOLOGY†
1983	TECHNOLOGY*	LARGE-CAP GROWTH
	small-cap companies	TECHNOLOGY†
	CYCLICALS	SMALL-CAP COMPANIES†
1984	ASSET PLAYS	CYCLICALS
		technology
		small-cap companies
1985‡	asset plays	

*First 6 months
†Second 6 months.
‡Through September 30, 1985.

69

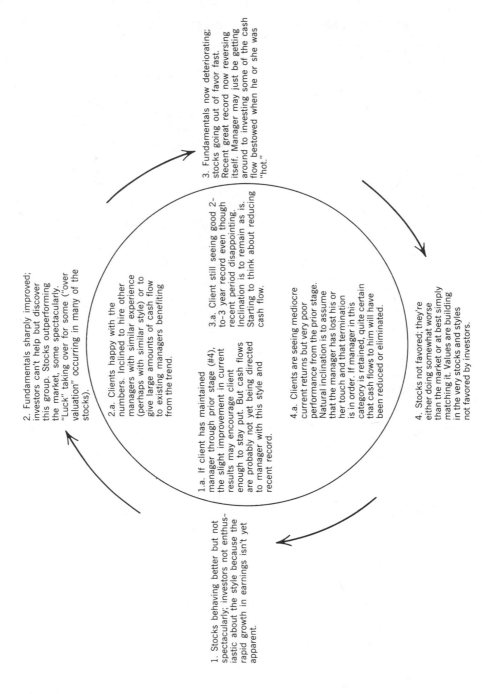

Figure 5.1 Client Guide 5. "The Endless Circle of Clients Zigging While Cycles Are Zagging."

2. Fundamentals sharply improved; investors can't help but discover this group. Stocks outperforming the market, some spectacularly. "Luck" taking over for some ("over valuation" occurring in many of the stocks).

2.a. Clients happy with the numbers. Inclined to hire other managers with similar experience (perhaps with similar style) or to give large amounts of cash flow to existing managers benefiting from the trend.

3. Fundamentals now deteriorating; stocks going out of favor fast. Recent great record now reversing itself. Manager may just be getting around to investing some of the cash flow bestowed when he or she was "hot."

3.a. Client still seeing good 2-to-3 year record even though recent period disappointing. Inclination is to remain as is. Starting to think about reducing cash flow.

1.a. If client has maintained manager through prior stage (#4), the slight improvement in current results may encourage client enough to stay put. But cash flows are probably not yet being directed to manager with this style and recent record.

4.a. Clients are seeing mediocre current returns but very poor performance from the prior stage. Natural inclination is to assume that the manager has lost his or her touch and that termination is in order. If manager in this category is retained, quite certain that cash flows to him will have been reduced or eliminated.

1. Stocks behaving better but not spectacularly; investors not enthusiastic about the style because the rapid growth in earnings isn't yet apparent.

4. Stocks not favored; they're either doing somewhat worse than the market or at best simply matching it. Values are building in the very stocks and styles not favored by investors.

likely to feel so secure that you will be inclined to direct cash flows *to* the action of the moment.

You certainly don't want to duplicate the experience of a major U.S. railroad. In 1970, this client fired its manager—a New York City bank invested mainly in large-capitalization growth stocks. The railroad shifted to a "value-oriented" manager, who sold Johnson & Johnson, Bristol-Myers, and similarly regarded growth stocks to invest in companies such as Exxon and General Motors, issues that then lagged the Nifty Fifty growth mania that persisted through 1972. The client couldn't weather its lagging participation in the growth surge, so in early 1973 it switched back to the very bank from which it had departed in 1971—in time for the latter to purchase Xerox, Disney, and some of the same securities that had been liquidated at significantly lower prices in 1971. By 1975, the client's round trip had cost over half the value of its total fund, a sad but true example of how *not* to play investment styles.

Barton M. Biggs, Morgan Stanley's astute portfolio strategist paraphrased a positive solution to our "endless circle," when in 1980 he wrote.

> If an investment officer really believes he has selected superior investment management firms that over five years will be in the top third of the manager universe, the rational strategy would be to take money from the firms that are in the top 20% over a two- or three-year market cycle and give more money to the firms that have underperformed. The theory is that, over time, top third managers will gravitate down and back up to that sustainable achievement level. My calculations indicate that with five managers and by making 20% additions and subtractions to the two worst and two best, respectively, the plan sponsor could add five to seven places to the overall fund's ranking in the fund universe over a five-year, two-market cycle. The opposite strategy of adding to the best and reducing the worst would subtract an equal number of ranking places. The riskiest approach would be to fire the low performers and hire new managers who have done well recently. Not only are there heavy transaction costs associated with the transfer from old to new, but also there is the strong possibility of firing a good manager at the bottom of his cycle and hiring a new manager at the top of his. Managers should be fired if their performance is bad over two full market cycles, roundly five years, or if the investment organization itself radically changes in terms of people or investment style.

George F. Russell, Jr., president of Frank Russell & Company consultants to pension fund managers, and described by *The Wall Street Journal* as "the most powerful person in the multibillion-dollar money management industry," echoes Bigg's statements. Russell says:

> If your bottom quartile managers were doing what you hired them to do and you still believe in their organizations and abilities . . . you should give them more money, because their stocks should be undervalued. If you reward last year's losers, consistently over time, you're going to make money.

Peter Bernstein, noted economist and editor of the *Journal of Portfolio Management*, puts it this way: "The client is generally wrong to fire a manager when the manager's style is out of favor. He should have left when the manager's style was in great favor and yet he failed to sell many of his stocks."

As Bernstein suggests, inflexible manager style is not to be condoned. Managers allowing extreme overvaluation of their securities to go unnoticed are not to be commended (nor perhaps retained). Performance comparisons of managers with similar styles (their "peer group") are useful to determine how poorly any one manager is doing. (More on this in Chapter 11.)

CONCLUSIONS

Client Guide 5 may seem exaggerated and somewhat jaded. It is not meant to reflect all client actions, or perhaps even most. You may not recognize yourself or your organization at all, in which case, as they say, "If it ain't broke, don't fix it." You may, however, have been spared the experience thus far but may be slated to face it sometime. The circle delineates very natural tendencies of both markets and clients—and it serves to remind you how important it is to have a practical knowledge of investment styles and cycles. Adjusting correctly to the circle and matching recent market experience with manager styles (Client Guide 4) should prepare you well for the cold, cruel world of investment manager choice.

6

IF YOU DOUBT THAT YOU CAN BEAT THE MARKET, WHY NOT SIMPLY JOIN IT? OR DO YOU NEED A MANAGER AT ALL?

'Tis better to have loved and lost
than never to have loved at all.

Sir Alfred Lord Tennyson
In Memoriam XXVII

About 25 years ago, a new investment theory emerged that has caused as much debate as anything considered for the prior 40 or 50 years. This theory has numerous names, including modern capital theory, modern portfolio theory, and efficient market hypothesis. All these propound that stock markets are "efficient"—that is, that across a broad spectrum of securities there is no knowledge or judgment an investor can add beyond what other investors have already (efficiently) perceived. As with all theories, there are degrees of fanaticism among the proponents of modern portfolio theory (MPT), but the staunchest advocates insist that there is so much efficiency that few investment managers can over time produce returns greater than the S&P 500 Stock Index (which is their proxy for the market). Efficient market practitioners are, of course, not saying that all investors will end up in the middle of the pack every year. In any given period, there will be the overachievers and underachievers. Over time, however, they insist that, just as water seeks its own level, most investors are slated to return to the level of the S&P. These advocates further reason that investment management fees are such a heavy additional burden that clients ought not to seek traditional advisers at all. They contend that "active" managers are unnecessary and that clients are better off following what is known today as "passive" management.

Passive management is accomplished through "indexing," which is simply a duplication* of the S&P 500. Because this duplication is normally mechanical, with no research or portfolio management decision makers involved, costs are insignificant—leading to very low client fees. Whereas active management fees range anywhere from a low of about 0.25 to as high as around 2 percent annually, charges for participating in an index fund are normally 0.1 percent or lower. Just as Robert Hall Clothiers used to advertise, "Why pay for overhead when you can't wear it," the indexing proponents are saying that investing clients are spending needless money for active management.

Another client burden to be saved through indexing (according to MPT proponents) is the potentially high commission and transaction

---

*Most indexers contend that precise duplication is unnecessary—that less than 500 securities can be selected from within the S&P without significant deviation of results from the index itself.

costs of active portfolio turnover. Commission and transaction costs naturally vary from manager to manager, however. Some investors hold securities for very long periods of time and experience relatively low penalties of this sort. Other managers have high portfolio turnover and experience high costs. This is not to imply that the buy-and-hold strategy is consistently more productive than more active portfolio structuring. While buy-and-hold worked well for many investors for portions of the 1950s and 1960s, this strategy was, for the most part, less successful in the 1970s and has been so thus far in the 1980s. Security selection and timing—the backbone of good portfolio management—normally require change, which in turn requires at least moderate activity and the related costs. With or without trading costs, efficient market proponents simply conclude that "the system" is operating against you—hence you ought not to fight it. Distressing as it may seem to serious investors to utilize a gambling analogy, the staunch MPT advocates are telling you to "bet with the house."

The obstacles to client success were well articulated by Charles Ellis in his treatise entitled "The Loser's Game." Ellis contended quite provocatively that investors are now working so skillfully that success is less dependent on being smart and aggressive and more on not losing and making mistakes. The really important thing, according to Ellis, is to shift from trying to beat other managers and the market towards the productive work of setting and holding to sound long-term policy.

As you can imagine, there is sharp disagreement about the market efficiency thesis. The S&P was formidable opposition for most managers in the early 1970s; then, from the mid-1970s through 1982, the S&P 500 *underperformed* active managers fairly substantially; and then in 1983 and 1984, managers lost to the S&P again. In recent years, numerous statistical studies poked additional holes in the indexing argument, and even some of its staunchest supporters raised doubts. In a recent issue of *Institutional Investor* magazine, an article by Julie Rohrer entitled "Ferment in Academia"* listed many original advocates, along with current academics and practitioners, who now seriously question or refute the

*Julie Rohrer, "Ferment in Academia," *Institutional Investor*, August 1985, pp. 69–78.

theory of market efficiency. "Evidence of academia," the article states, "mounts against [it]."

The vast majority of investment professionals have refuted the theory. This, of course, is to be expected. After all, egos and reputations and many very profitable businesses are endangered by the threat of indexing. Countless investment managers, particularly those who have handsomely beaten the S&P over the years, have explained why they consider the theory incorrect. Arthur Zeikel, president of Merrill Lynch Asset Management, Inc., and a member of the editorial board of the *Financial Analysts Journal*, made an interesting observation in 1983 when he stated:

> The accepted definition of efficiency is inaccurate because it does not describe well how the market's pricing mechanism actually works. That is, the market is efficient, in that current price generally reflects the consensus view of investor expectations for the market as a whole and for most individual issues. But the consensus view is usually incorrect, because it is based on a more or less simple extrapolation of past trends and events and does not effectively incorporate change into expectations.

In a way, therefore, the argument is similar to how one perceives the half-filled glass of water: Is it half empty or half full? The stock market is a mechanism in which investors vote their opinions daily, and they can do so democratically. The great nineteenth-century American author James Fennimore Cooper stated that the "tendency of democracies is, in all things, to mediocrity." Indexers are content to be in the middle of the pack, while Zeikel and countless others contend that this very mediocrity only represents opportunity for the superior managers.

There are many other thoughts about efficient markets and indexing. For example:

1.   The S&P index itself is not without human interference. Companies no longer in existence because of mergers are naturally excluded, but stocks representing companies that have fallen on very bad times are often deleted and replaced by more successful entities. Isn't this selling at the bottom and buying at the top? the critics cry.

2.   Over the last 12 years, S&P has made several hundred changes in its index, thereby proving that human interference (just like active portfolio management) exists and causing transaction costs to index holders.

3.   Strong criticism emanates from what index investing entails. As individual securities rise in price, their representation within the S&P rises, too—as do, of course, industry representations. For example, the sharp rise in energy stocks from 1975 to 1980 enticed index buyers into owning more and more of a group that was becoming seriously overpriced and that ultimately constituted over 30 percent of the S&P. Many serious investors question the wisdom and prudence of having investment exposure of this magnitude in *any* group. Is this really "medium risk," as the theory implies? Isn't the indexed investor in this case exposed to significant potential loss of capital, which is how high risk is best defined?

4.   Investors who believe that one should buy more of a security as its price declines (thereby receiving more value per dollar of investment), as well as urging more caution as market prices advance, scoff at a technique that encourages the opposite posture.

5.   Some MPT advocates point to the growing and dominant position of institutions within the marketplace as further proof that investors cannot outperform over time. They assume that the sophistication of large investors will produce low prices for the weaker stocks and high prices for the stronger ones, leaving no "edge" for anyone. A strong counterargument to this is that size hardly guarantees sophistication, acumen, or investment success. As a matter of fact, size presents numerous problems: It can limit the securities that might be owned; it can complicate finding adequate investment management talent; and it can lead to herd instincts, which have spelled trouble for investors over the many years of investment history. Furthermore, institutional activity has been virtually nonexistent in options markets, which attract large trading activity and which influence pricing of securities in the very markets in which institutions are so dominant. Hence, many institutions are fighting a war without full weaponry.

6.   Although indexers ultimately expect absolute rates of return from investing in their market proxy, major emphasis is on relative results. It is

hardly comforting for an investor to be told that he should be satisfied with negative returns of, say, 20 percent in some given year just because that is what the S&P produced. If assumptions about the S&P are outdated—if the index is not slated to grow as well as other proxies—investors are tying their fate to a falling rather than a rising star.

7.   Part of the statistical evidence against professional managers exceeding the market stems from the "lackadaisical" period of investment counsel referred to in Chapter 2. Prior to the early 1970s, the managers were mainly banks and "slower, less competitive" advisers. As one client remarked recently: "The S&P sure had easy 'foes' in those days!"

Since volumes of work would be required to carry the argument of efficient versus inefficient markets to a satisfactory conclusion, the above is intended as a base for you. Superior managers will always exist, and the purpose of this book is to help you recognize them. This does not mean that indexing constitutes an evil; it may be a sensible approach for some investors. Very large funds, for example, are logical users of indexing—if they cannot find enough managers they feel confident will outperform the market. Likewise, clients who find that significant portions of their managed portfolios remain essentially indexed anyway—for example, they find that industry holdings and individual stock positions regularly parallel the S&P 500—may just as well utilize a lower-cost, indexed approach for some part of their assets.

From a positive viewpoint, some investors have utilized index funds as low-cost vehicles for market timing, contending that they can easily shift back and forth between cash and the funds. Studies on market timing per se and on institutional (mis-)timing in particular hardly support this use of indexing. There is no reason, however, why an index cannot be assessed on a supply/demand basis, as other investments are. Astute investors might take advantage of the cycles of indexing just as they do in individual securities.

Thus, indexing is a logical approach for any of the following investor types: (1) those who can time general market swings; (2) those who cannot seem to get away from being essentially indexed in their active management and/or those who cannot get adequate attention to their needs; (3) those who are not likely to choose the overachievers, including mutual fund buyers likely to make poor fund selections; or (4) those who recognize that their own client actions are likely to inhibit success in the future. In short, if you doubt you can "beat the market," you can "join it" through passive management.

Not intended as a practice manual on MPT, this chapter at least presents the basic arguments on active and passive management. For those who embrace Tennyson's philosophy about *trying*, this book prepares you to *find and keep the excellent managers who will exceed market returns and produce superior results over time.*

PART 2

PIERCING THE VEIL:

How to Judge
Manager Talent
Before You Hire

ENTERING THE INNER SANCTUM OF INVESTMENT PERFORMANCE

There are lies, damn lies,
and statistics.

Disraeli

The handwriting on the wall
may be a forgery.

Ralph Hodgson
America in Our Time

Numbers in any field can be deceptive. They can be inaccurate and they can be—and frequently are—manipulated. Despite this, people are tempted to seek correlations from them, most of which involve dangerous extrapolations of patterns that are seldom slated to repeat themselves.

These caveats are especially true in investing, whether the attempt is to forecast security prices or to choose the investment manager winners of the future. Dangers exist for clients for two major reasons. First, most people are vulnerable because they prefer simplistic explanations—and numbers *appear* more conclusive than "softer" inputs. This tendency is too often encouraged by the more aggressive managers and by certain consultants who feed on manager turnover (and who design performance scoreboards as the backbone of their services). As Ameritech's Don Phillips says,

> Consultants' performance tabulations are too often presented as a fancy "speedometer" which looks tangible to the client and helps to sell the consultant's service. Concentration from then on focuses on this—on the speedometer rather than on manager qualities, which are the equivalent of a car's motor. It's obviously the motor which is most important!

The second danger of performance numbers is the inexactness and, in may cases, the dishonesty involved. One way, therefore, to strengthen your client armor against dangerous manager thrusting is to "get behind" the numbers—to recognize flimsiness, to understand certain "tricks" being played, and to develop a sense of reality about the performance scoreboard. Indeed, too many important investment management decisions are based either on fragile data or on misinterpretations of reasonable data.

Poor statistics will lead to poor policies, but even the most legitimately gathered data and the best-intended extrapolations are open to serious question. Periods under study, whether they be 2, 5, 10, 20, or even 50 years, are not necessarily indicative of the future. As author Barbara Tuchman put it: "You cannot extrapolate any series in which the human element intrudes; history, that is, the human narrative never follows, and will always fool, the scientific curve."

In addition, the starting point for statistical studies—the base year(s)—

can create great biases. For instance, the most recent five decades reach from 1930 to 1980, certainly a questionable time period for investors to consider since it commenced with the stock market crash of 1929, followed by 10 years of the Great Depression, followed by 5 of World War II, and another 10 or so of governmental "fiddling" with interest rates (the "pegging" of rates from 1942 to 1952). With at least half the 50 years cluttered by such events, is it really logical to expect the conclusions to be applicable today?

The renowned Ibbotson-Sinquefield (I-S) studies of investment returns, which have become the basis for many investment decisions, show how rigid extrapolations can be misleading. The authors are serious, honest practitioners, and their data accumulation has provided a great service, but interpretations of the work need to be tempered by an understanding of the events mentioned above. The first of the I-S studies (which covered the period from to 1925 to 1975) suggested that intermediate and long-term bonds should "normally" yield 2 to 3 percent over the rate of inflation. Ironically—or perhaps typically—since the study's final year (1975) there has been no such discernible relationship between inflation and bond yields. Perhaps Winston Churchill helped investors when he said: "If we open a quarrel between the past and the present, we shall find that we have lost the future."

A very different statistical correlation was discovered by Robert Stovall, former director of investment policy for Dean Witter Reynolds. With tongue in cheek, but backed by facts, Stovall pored over mountains of data and finally concluded that the most reliable indicator of stock market behavior has been . . . whether an American or National Football Conference team wins the Super Bowl! (If the AFC team wins in January, the market will go down; if an NFC team wins, the market goes up!) This Super Bowl: Stock Market correlation has proved correct in 16 of the last 18 Super Bowl years, the only exceptions being when AFC representatives Kansas City (1970) and Los Angeles (formerly Oakland) (1984) won and the S&P rose a scant 0.1 percent and 1.4 percent respectively. There are thousands of other studies, most far more serious than this, that have gone down in flames over the years. Hope—and hopeful pundits—springs eternal, however.

This is not to say that economic or other history has no place in investment thinking. History can be especially useful because:

1.   The past serves as an important reminder of how *cycles persist*, an understanding that should help investors deal with the inevitable ups and downs of the future. When the philosopher George Santayana stated, "We are condemned to repeat history," he was referring to broad actions (such as cycles) rather than intricate specifics (such as precise investment relationships).

2.   The past is a guide to the inevitable volatility of performance figures, that is, proof that there is little semblance of accuracy over the short run and that only a longer-range view promises any hope of consistency. This understanding should prove reassuring through the trying periods, just as it should lead to the setting of more realistic objectives by investors. It should also throw cold water on unreasonable promises made to clients, something pointed out very sensibly by investment strategist and author Steve Leuthold. Leuthold made a great point when he rightfully criticized "claims now being made by some younger members of the venture capital crowd" in late 1983. Many of these venture capitalists were predicting returns of 25 to 35 percent compounded annually over the next 10 or 15 years, and Leuthold seriously questioned their claims by: (1) pointing to past experience of investment vehicles, which proves that no one type sustains dramatic returns for very long; and (2) indicating how grandiose 25 to 35 percent really is; for example, each $1 becoming between $28 and $51 for 25 and 35 percent assumptions, respectively, after 15 years. As Leuthold concluded about a pension fund officer who gave money to a particular venture capitalist based on the projected returns: "The pension officer either would buy the Brooklyn Bridge or *thinks* he owns it."

Thus, we can and should learn from history. But we should not expect exactness from it. And we should be wary of theories of all sorts, whether they are based on historical analogy or on mounds of data that you cannot possibly check for reliability or completeness.

Still, the acid test of money management clearly is performance. Both clients and managers have a natural interest in results, and both should know how to assess such results correctly. The investment industry has taken great pains to devise formulas and statistics that indicate how an account is faring and how managers compare with one another.

As commendable as this sounds, it will hardly surprise you to learn how much scrutiny, interpretation, and skepticism must be applied to performance numbers. Like the proverbial skeleton in the closet, a real-life understanding of performance has been hidden from those who need it most.

If there is an inner sanctum anywhere in investment management that needs investigation, it is performance statistics—which are both less exact than they appear and too often riddled with dishonesty! So let us open the squeaky door and provide light where there is darkness, and let us find out how to make intelligent moves based on *more* realistic numbers.

In case you are worried about being bombarded with complicated equations and higher mathematics, relax. A few simple illustrations will be presented, but there will be no accounting-type intricacies.

A FEW SIMPLE FACTS ABOUT PERFORMANCE NUMBERS

To start, you should constantly remind yourself that performance numbers must be considered approximations. The old adage about real estate—"You never know the true value of a property until you have cashed the check from the sale"—applies to values placed on publicly traded securities, too. Though stocks and bonds trade with greater liquidity than real estate (quoted prices on securities reflect actual daily sales), even stock and bond prices possess an element of softness since they are not adjusted for size. If the last sale of IBM is $120, you can certainly sell 100 or 1000 or perhaps even 10,000 shares within a close proximity to the $120 price. However, if you own 200,000 shares, you probably face a different situation. And trying to sell 200,000 IBM shares may be simple compared to selling a mere 5000 shares of some thinly traded security lacking IBM-type liquidity: The price will sag at the very hint of such selling pressure. The same thing is true of fixed-income securities. Treasury obligations are extremely liquid, but buying and selling costs can be affected by size, too.* Lower-quality corporate or utility obligations (and most municipal bonds) normally lack great marketability; their last sale prices may be no more realistic than the hypothetical 5000-share sale price of the thinly traded stock example above.

This is not to imply that softness in quoted prices renders performance numbers meaningless. The stated values are usually close enough to reality to provide an adequate measure of results. There are other, more serious factors that can affect performance figures. Leaving aside some technical complications (i.e., cash versus accrual accounting, or the use of trade dates versus settlement dates), one common problem involves the many times when a manager's reported performance fails to match the apparent dollar results of the client. Differences such as this can imply dishonest manager reporting, but much of the time they are merely a result of different accounting methods. For example, you may be evaluating the absolute dollar changes in your portfolio, while your manager may be evaluating the same results adjusted for the timing of cash flows. Such confusion usually stems from the differences between dollar-weighted and time-weighted performance accounting. Although dollar-weighted accounting gives the exact rate earned on funds invested, time weighting is the only really useful method for comparing the performance of two portfolio managers, since it essentially neutralizes the impact of cash flows in and out of an account and realistically reflects the manager's results. It is therefore the method you will have to depend on in practically all cases.

An example will illustrate the differences in the two methods. Assume that you gave me $100,000 to manage and that exactly 12 months later the combination of income earned and increased capital boosts the value of the account to exactly $200,000. Because your account started with one amount of money and has had no additions or withdrawals, my report to you, based on time-weighted calculations, shows a performance of

---

*A "barbell" effect is common, with relative costs highest for very small amounts of money and then next highest for amounts that are so large as to affect supply/demand relationships in the markets.

+100.00 percent—exactly what your dollar-based calculations tell you is correct. You are so pleased with the results that you now decide to add $2 million to my management*, bringing your account to $2.2 million.

The next year isn't nearly so productive, however, and your account loses 10 percent. (I earn some income for you, but this is overshadowed by a decrease in the market value of securities in your portfolio.) The 10 percent net loss has reduced your $2.2 million by $220,000 to $1.98 million. As a result, you calculate that my net performance over the 2-year period is −5.7 percent, based on these figures:

Your original capital	$ 100,000
Your added capital	2,000,000
Your total invested capital	2,100,000
Your value today	1,980,000
Final result:	Loss of $120,000 divided by original invested capital of $2,100,000 = −5.71%

My time-weighted performance report to you unfortunately differs sharply from this dollar-weighted calculation. It shows not −5.7 percent, but +80 percent, figured as follows:

The increase of $100,000 on your first $100,000 took your starting index number of 100.00 to 200.00. An increase of 100.00 on the 100.00 base equals a 100 % increase for the year.

The loss of $220,000 on base of $2.2 million in year two takes your 200.00 index down 20.00 points (down 10 %) to 180.00.

Net performance over the 2 years is the 80.00 points over the 100.00 starting point (80.00 ÷ 100.00) equals +80.00%.

Both dollar weighting and time weighting have their advantages and drawbacks. While dollar weighting is more useful for comparing absolute

---

*Hopefully your reading about cycles and styles in Chapter 5 would have cautioned you. There may have been abnormal reasons for the 100 percent bonanza.

dollar results with specific goals, it is misleading because it implies that investment decision making can be isolated from the timing of cash flows. In fact, the size of contributions or withdrawals from an account can have an overwhelming impact on performance—in many cases much greater impact than investment decision making itself.

Looking again at our illustration, if you had added another $100,000 (instead of $2 million) to your $200,000 balance after the first year, and if I had then incurred the same 10 percent loss, your dollar-weighted performance report would have changed dramatically. Instead of your −5.7 percent calculation, the dollar-weighted result would have shown as +35.0 percent, as follows:

Your original capital	$100,000
Your added capital	100,000
Your total invested capital	200,000
Your value today	270,000

(Your original $100,000 plus the 100% first-year gain of $100,000 equals $200,000, plus $100,000 capital addition equals $300,000, which declines by 10%, or $30,000, equals $270,000.)

Final result: Your $70,000 gain
divided by original
invested capital of
$200,000 equals +35.0%

My +100 percent and −10 percent efforts were identical, and yet the dollar-weighted performance differences were huge (−5.7 versus +35.0 percent)—all because of amounts and timing of cash flows beyond my control. You can imagine how cash flows, which are bound to vary both in size and duration from client to client, render dollar-weighted comparisons of managers virtually meaningless. In contrast, time-weighted results will not be affected by the cash flow variables (with one major exception, to be covered later in this chapter).

Despite their limitations, time-weighted calculations are usually the most reflective of a manager's decision making. They are normally all you can use for manager comparisons, unless you are judging a small group managing identical sums with identical cash flows.

Let's now proceed to more penetrating explorations of the inner sanctum, designed to protect you from many investment manager and consultant abuses.

ELIMINATING THE "FLUFF" OF PERFORMANCE NUMBERS

If Disraeli's opinion of statistics is valid, you can be sure that performance statistics qualify as among the very worst prevarications. The burden of proof is definitely on those counting on the past to predict future investment results.

Time now to enter the inner sanctum of investment performance—through seven caveats to be assimilated by anyone interested in judging investment records, either past or present, plus Manager Queries intended to expose any fluff that might exist in these records.

Always Account for Size When Assessing Performance

Size is acknowledged to be a problem in the investment business. Everyone agrees that, the more money involved, the greater the problems of marketability, ability to structure portfolios, openness to certain dynamic, small-growth investing, and so on. People disagree about which size levels constitute serious detriments to investment performance. And for good reason, because any size threshold is a function of manager style and periodic, changing market preferences. Threshold amounts are obviously far lower for a manager who stresses owning small companies than for a manager dealing mainly in large companies. And the character of markets makes a difference, too: heavy-volume trading markets do not restrict larger managers as much as light-volume conditions do.

Regardless of style or markets, all management firms face a challenge to prove that their clients will prosper in the future as they have in the past. Can they produce similar results for their clients as their assets under management grow from $10 million to $50 million, $50 million to $500 million, $1 billion to $3 billion?

Why, then, don't managers indicate size of assets next to their performance figures?

The answer is a mystery, although the void certainly persists because clients have not demanded more information. Wisdom, therefore, demands that *all performance data include size of assets managed alongside each performance period.* If there is a significant divergence between results when assets were tiny and results when they were large, it will be immediately obvious—and it is worth consideration by you.

Here, then, is the **Manager Query** for you to pose:

Manager Query: *Show me your total client assets under management for each period of your investment management, along with your performance results.*

Separate Out Unrepresentative Performance Where It Exists

Ignoring size may be an innocent oversight by both clients and managers. The same should not be said about the use of *unrepresentative* numbers utilized by many managers and by some consulting organizations.

Believe it or not, some people point to fictitious portfolio examples (so-called paper portfolios that do not represent actual transactions) as representative, whereas any investment professional will tell you these are poor proxies for reality. Some managers, many writers of investment letters, those who experiment with systems, and others, for example, often construct lists of securities recommended for purchase or sale from which they calculate "results." The calculations are more informative than no assessment at all, but these paper portfolios seldom, if ever, properly account for execution and transaction costs (for buying and selling), and they *never* allow for the entirely different "emotional stress" involved in actual "hard dollar" management.

Equally inexcusable is the paucity of investment advisers who have constructed true composites of their performance results—composites that include returns for every dollar under management over every period. Incidentally, "every dollar" should mean exactly that—including accounts no longer under a firm's management. As you can imagine, there is a huge potential difference between a composite of all accounts and those results that are often emphasized by managers as "representative." Cynical though it may sound, you should assume that an account labeled "representative" is most likely to be a manager's very best or near best. Alas, comparing one manager's all-inclusive performance composite against another manager's chosen "representative" accounts is not only comparing apples to oranges; it is comparing apples to "illusory oranges."

Composite figures have their complications, too, since client objectives, risks taken, size, and other factors can vary widely. Thus you need to be told the source of these numbers, just as you would any others. Although you should be skeptical of practically all numbers, composites should be vastly superior gauges, particularly when

1. Different composites are available for managed equity accounts versus bond accounts versus balanced portfolios.

2. Taxable and nontaxable accounts are separated.

3. Fully discretionary (where manager has free rein) accounts are distinguished from nondiscretionary data.

4. Distinctions can be made for varying risks assumed. For example, a manager whose investment style is medium risk but who also manages specialized high-technology, small-capitalization stock portfolios should have composites for each.

5. The range of results for all accounts in each category are divulged. Wide variances in performance should be explained.

Ideally, performance data should be audited. If not, managers should include language of assurance that the figures are all-inclusive and that the calculations are legitimate.

Despite the difficulties of assembling totally pristine performance figures, *composites that include every like account ever managed in every year are decidedly superior to all other manager figures. You have a right to full disclosure, and you should demand such composites.*

Manager Query: Show me performance results for every account ever managed by you with objectives and characteristics similar to mine. Tell me specifically how many of your accounts (including dollars involved) have been included in and excluded from these performance calculations.

Seeing Through Potentially "Warped" Larger Samples of Manager Results

If one enlightened overlord of performance results were to exist, composites like those just explained would be mandatory. Since this omnipotent being has yet to appear, many clients and consultants have stepped in to fill the gap by compiling their own data on manager results. Unfortunately, most of the indices they have constructed are fraught with problems, too. Good intent has been spoiled by inadequate stringency, and in many cases the supposedly objective samples have become almost as warped as what many managers submit themselves. In fact, wide disparities exist within consultants' indices. A 1984 "Money Management Letter" highlighted the "debate among consultants as to whose figures are the most meaningful." The median results of 12 sets of consultant-compiled performance data for 1983 ran the gamut from 18.0 to 21.4 percent—a spread "perhaps 2–3 times what even most of the same consultants considered a statistical aberration."

Just as you have to delve below the surface in manager-presented results, therefore, you have to probe the sources, the breadth, and the depth of others' compilations. How can you separate truly meaningful performance samples from others? By following these rules:

1. Insist on the broadest samples. If compilations contain but a few of each manager's accounts, breadth is inadequate and data are likely to be *unrepresentative.*

2. Make sure that the sample contains verified inputs. I know of one case where a very prestigious management firm submitted bond performance with returns from cash equivalents set aside for *equity*

purchases. The year had not been a good one for longer-maturity bonds, so the cash equivalents added to their results. In this case, the consultant discovered the wide disparities between the firm's actual bond accounts and their submitted data, but it's a certainty that most of this kind of cheating goes unnoticed. If managers have been allowed to submit *their* selected data, *and* if the figures are not confirmed, a potential fox has been placed in charge of the chicken coop!

3. Determine how much data come from actual experience as opposed to after-the-fact presentation. A sample that mixes manager A's actual results with client B's money over the past 10 years along with manager C's data submitted in 1985 (for the same 10 years) is open to question. As mentioned, C's presentation is likely to be representative of his *best* performing accounts, not of a composite.

4. Determine whether any manager results have been altered at any time.*

5. Assess any efforts made to differentiate the varying risks taken by the different managers in the sample.

Whether you are questioning large samples compiled by supposedly objective individuals or the results of an individual manager, your very best ploy comes from concentrating on *omission*. Indeed, *knowing what has been left out can provide the best clues.* Many managers have a host of separate funds and yet present only the convenient ones that they rationalize as being "pertinent to objectives" to either prospective clients or compilers of samples.

Amazingly, it wasn't until March 4, 1985, that I observed any publicized awareness of pooled fund proliferation practiced by many managers. Randall Smith, staff reporter for *The Wall Street Journal*, wrote about how many "mutual fund managers seem to manufacture track records like cars on an assembly line." Smith insists that they can keep it

---

*As Caroline Cummings, former director of investment manager research at Meidinger Asset Planning Services, stated: "Managers who systematically submit and update performance results for consultants frequently change historical results." Cummings cites an example of a firm that in 1981 revised its 1980 equity results from +15 percent to +30 percent after a key portfolio manager departed. Indices allowing such nonsense should obviously be discarded by clients.

(a new fund) small, "pack it with new issues . . . to pump up perfor-mance," and then, when a fund experiences "a torrid track record, the company enthusiastically promotes it to the general public." Smith fur-ther states, "Little, if any, of that kind of orchestration is disclosed," implying (wisely) that investors are being deceived and that what you see is hardly what you get.

If you don't see everything, you might end up like the horse players taken advantage of by Bob Hope in the comedy *The Lemon Drop Kid.* Hope played the part of a tout who recommended a series of different horses in the same race to a series of bettors. The result was expensive for both the toutees whose horses lost and those whose horses won and who then gave Hope more money for his advice on future bets.

You can see then how even the best-intended samples can be "warped." And you can understand again why all-inclusive, pertinent composites make the best sense.

Manager (or Consultant) Query: Explain exactly how your data have been assembled, particularly which of every manager's results have not been included.

Look Behind the Figures for "Less-Deserved" Profits

Periods exist when investors are graced with "gifts" from the new issue* market—times when new issues of stocks or convertible bonds are gob-bled up and sent to immediate premiums as occurred with tulip bulbs in seventeenth-century Holland. These fads (frenzies) seldom last more than 6 to 12 months. They have appeared in the late 1960s and several times since then (the latest in early 1983). The fact that the fads soon self-destruct suggests to some that those who end up net winners must possess skills and that the profits *are* as deserved as any others.

The refutation of this is that a wild new-issue market can create sufficient profits to offset what might be lost later. Remember, these "hot" phases allow investors to buy and sell securities essentially the same

---

*Often referred to as IPO (initial public offering).

day—for large percentage gains. If one is early enough in the cycle, if one has access to broker/underwriter distribution, and particularly if one is small enough at the time to enable these windfalls to produce significant impact on one's accounts, a manager can build an enticing record. (Once the new-issue market cools off, it will not take much genius to back away and simply not "play" any more.)

This is not meant to be a bitter tirade against all who participate in these occasional manias. It does take insight to recognize such trends at their outset; it should be encouraging for you to know that your manager is paying attention to smaller, interesting companies; and it is reassuring to know that your account is not forgotten during such periods. Furthermore, discrimination is required—not all the new issues rise, and some obviously rise far more than others.

But the skills required are hardly of the same caliber as consistently wise purchasing and selling of securities in which profits are not presented on a silver platter. When a new-issue craze is in full swing, buying mainly requires an inkling of what the "opening price" will approximate, something which in the wildest periods is better done through opinions from broker trading desks (who get a feeling for demand for shares prior to the offering) than through the more reliable manager approach of defining value. To borrow from basketball, the new-issue craze is an undefended layup as opposed to a skillful maneuver against a strong defense.

Since skillful maneuvering is what is required more than 95 percent of the time in investing, the "gifts" should hardly be accorded the credits for managerial know-how that you should rely on over time. To turn back to our basketball example, shouldn't you know whether your "player" has performed under rigid playing conditions rather than piling up points in the fantasy of solitary practice?

Don't count on managers to admit that performance has been enhanced by gifts. Very few, if any, project the humility of John F. Kennedy, who, when asked how he became a war hero, said: "It was involuntary. They sank my boat."

It is amazing that clients, consultants, or others have not insisted that *managers quantify the effect that new issues have had on performance during any period.* Organizations sporting fancy numbers built almost solely on such conditions exist today—and more will emerge sometime in the future. Hundreds of millions of dollars have been shifted by clients not aware of these flimsy, one-time-performance spectaculars. So the plea is obvious. Managers should publicly quantify the effect of all new issues so that clients can assess the genesis—and the true "genius"—of their performance. And you should insist on such information!

Although not near so flimsy as new issue profits, clients should be aware of performance bonanzas from buy-outs/mergers of stocks in a manager's portfolio. Greater analytical skills are generally involved in isolating these potential values, but luck can play a big role in the timing and price realization, too.

> *Manager Query: Indicate (again) the size of accounts used in your sample, along with specific impact of new-issue or other "special" profits during each period.*

Determine Whether Cash Flow Abnormalities Affected Reported Figures

Performance anomalies can derive from other circumstances beyond a manager's control. Managers who receive large cash inflows from new accounts, or very large sums from existing accounts, will normally "average" their way into the market. They seldom will put all new monies to work at once, for a variety of reasons. The performance consequences of this conservatism, however, can be surprising. If the markets are volatile at the time of the cash contributions or withdrawals, the performance numbers are likely to be influenced by a quirk that can result from time-weighted calculations. As managers, consultants, and bank custodians shift to *daily* allocations of cash flows, this confusion will disappear, but cash infusions have in the past made and probably will continue to make a manager look much better in declining markets and much worse in rising markets. (The reverse—results from cash withdrawals—is obviously also true.) Because of these potentials, the onus is on you to search for such abnormalities so that you can better assess a manager's worth.

Admittedly, performance distortions resulting from cash flows are difficult to ascertain and quantify. However, hard questioning—with specific probing of a manager's cash flow experience during particularly volatile markets—can be sufficient detective work to produce a "feel" for the substance of his performance numbers.

Manager Query: Please document cash infusions from new or existing accounts in each of the past 10 years or so. (Then you, the client, should compare these with the experience of general markets in the years of extreme movements, attempting to identify possible "lucky" and "unlucky" periods.)

Analyze How Else Performance Evolved—Look at Style and Specific Holdings

In Chapter 10, you will be shown additional ways to determine whether a manager has made money by well-conceived reasoning or by exceptional luck, but it is an important enough issue to be discussed here as well. A manager who bought XYZ stock for its technological advances in genetics only to see this fail and who benefits from some very farfetched event (oil discovered on a property) hardly deserves the accolades owing to the investor whose reasoning behind ownership proves sound. The same approach can be taken to losses. Is the manager who owned Union Carbide, which suffered the disastrous chemical leak in India in 1984, as culpable as the owner of Warner Communications, who should have known that Atari was suffering market share deterioration and related operating losses in 1982? Yes, luck can have a bearing on results, and clients should attempt to differentiate this from sound analysis.

Probing here is not easy, since a prospective client doesn't have experience with the manager to consider; existing clients have to listen intently and dig deeply to make such judgments. But then most of the hurdles to accurate assessment require either a change in industry standards (let's hope that managers begin volunteering the information called for here) or stronger client demands for more straightforward inputs.

One way better to understand a manager's moves is to analyze his stock holdings, grouped by industry segments, over the past 1, 2, 3, 5, or more years (probably best shown on a quarterly or semiannual basis). Client Guide 6 illustrates this.

CLIENT GUIDE 6
Changes in Account by Industry

	Percentage in Account 12/31/80	Percentage in Account 6/30/81	Percentage in Account 12/31/81	Percentage in Account 6/30/82	Percentage in Account 12/31/82	Percentage in Account 6/30/83	Percentage in Account 12/31/83	Percentage in Account 6/30/84	Percentage in Account 12/31/84
Cash	2.5	2.9	1.3	4.2	7.8	5.8	6.8	6.6	2.2
Bonds	—	—	—	—	—	—	—	—	—
General finance	1.5	1.6	—	—	2.5	4.6	1.1	3.2	0.5
Banking	2.0	2.1	2.1	—	—	—	1.4	—	—
Insurance	3.5	3.5	3.0	15.1	6.8	4.0	3.4	4.1	5.9
Utilities	2.5	2.6	2.8	—	—	—	—	2.3	7.2
Energy—oil	30.5	28.2	28.5	22.2	16.8	4.2	8.8	8.7	4.0
Energy—non-oil	—	—	3.4	—	—	—	—	—	—
Raw materials	2.5	2.8	2.5	2.1	1.1	4.2	3.5	1.1	1.9
Chemicals—textiles	2.0	1.8	2.2	4.3	4.1	6.8	5.9	4.5	3.6
Containers	—	—	—	—	—	—	—	—	—
Building/construction	—	—	—	—	—	2.3	1.9	1.3	1.3

Transportation service	—	4.2	—	—	—	1.8	3.8	3.7	4.5
Industrial equipment/machinery	4.0	—	—	—	—	2.1	3.3	2.1	2.0
Electrical equipment	3.5	—	5.4	—	—	—	—	2.0	4.5
Transportation equipment	11.0	10.2	2.1	—	—	—	1.5	6.7	4.0
Auto related	—	—	—	—	—	2.4	2.7	2.0	—
Consumer durables	—	—	—	—	—	—	—	2.2	2.4
Beverage/tobacco	—	2.0	5.6	—	2.3	2.6	2.2	3.3	4.0
Food, food processing	—	—	—	—	—	—	—	—	—
Retail/wholesale	3.0	2.9	3.0	3.0	—	1.5	1.6	3.3	3.4
Household/nondurables	3.0	7.8	7.9	8.0	5.1	5.6	0.9	2.6	2.3
Health/drugs	3.0	2.2	7.3	8.0	12.2	7.8	8.9	6.2	7.2
Leisure time	3.0	2.5	1.7	5.1	5.8	2.5	5.6	2.8	1.2
Business/food service	5.0	3.7	5.0	3.1	5.1	3.3	1.3	2.6	7.1
Communications	3.5	4.1	6.5	7.0	3.4	5.8	4.4	5.4	6.0
Computer/office equipment	3.0	3.5	2.1	4.7	8.0	8.1	7.2	2.5	6.2
Electronics/technical	3.0	—	—	—	4.6	10.5	8.3	5.0	3.2
Small-cap growth stocks	11.0	11.4	9.4	13.2	14.4	14.1	15.6	15.9	15.4
	100.0%	100.0%	100.0%	100.0%	100.0%	100.0%	100.0%	100.0%	100.0%

The guide provides a synopsis of potentially useful information. The cash line indicates how active the manager has been in market timing. (This particular manager has been inactive, with a maximum of 7.8 percent cash position over the 5 years.) If cash positions have varied widely and reached substantial proportions at any time, you can compare the high and low percentages against general market highs and lows to assess the manager's proficiency at this timing strategy.

The industry information (percentages in each group in each of the reporting periods) provides a picture of your manager's style and strategies. If he owns all groups, you might question his conviction. Is he really a "closet indexer" who is essentially duplicating the market while charging a nonindex fee (as described in Chapter 6)?

The bold print numbers in the guide highlight the manager's most significant changes and industry strategy moves. You can learn a lot by comparing the largest and smallest positions against related industry gains or losses for various periods. Concentrating on the most significant industry trends can also be meaningful; for example, note how the account was 32.0 percent in energy—oil at the end of 1980 but was still over 28 percent throughout 1981 while that group was plummeting. (Although it is always possible that some positive performance from individual stocks within the energy group kept the percentage holdings high, your probing would no doubt have indicated the opposite.) Tracking this group's holdings through ensuing years would give you one (admittedly isolated, but perhaps meaningful) indication of the manager's abilities in this one industry group, his concentration of your dollars and the relative risks incurred this way, and his willingness to change. The fact that he finally exited the energy group only in 1983, just prior to a decent performance time for certain oil stocks, should be equally meaningful. In short, your manager's basic style, specific strategic moves, and the derivation of his performance results become much clearer through the guide. If nothing else, it is a method vastly superior to poring over mountains of reports.

A good illustration of how this can be helpful to manager assessment occurred in the mid-1970s. I know of several management firms that had bought "old-line industrial America" (International Harvester, duPont,

General Motors, Bethlehem and U.S. Steel) in the 1960s and stayed with these securities for 5, 10, or even more years of dismal operating (and stock market) results. Many years later, Wall Street finally became enchanted with what was termed "pricing power"—a belief that these industrial giants, despite being in mature industries and despite being saddled in many cases with questionable managerial capabilities, were entering a more favorable supply/demand period. Even though the industries promised little unit growth, enthusiasm reigned about a surge in profitability.

These "smokestack" stocks suddenly outperformed other industry groups, and numerous managers, whose judgment of past fundamentals had been deplorable and who seemingly had closed their eyes to portfolio change, suddenly experienced excellent results. This only lasted for about 2 years (1975 and 1976), but the emerging performance numbers were enough to turn the heads of many new clients, who should have based their hiring decisions on more information. Similar experience occurred in the bond market in 1982; those who had unwisely clung for years to long-maturity bonds finally had a field day.

To guard against choosing managers of less skill than their recent performance numbers suggest, you should learn to differentiate among: (1) managers who follow a well-articulated style (e.g., of owning cyclical stocks through thick and thin); (2) managers who shift portfolio holdings to a group, such as the cyclicals just prior to their emergence; and (3) managers who make poor judgments and are unwilling to recognize their mistakes.

Even the first category of manager is open to question. Should any one-style stock advocate, no matter how devoted and how well he has explained his philosophy, cause his clients to suffer as long as cyclical stock owners had to? Should the growth stock advocates of the very early 1970s be commended for clinging to a drastically overvalued group? You should hardly be expected to have this much patience.

Certainly managers in the last category deserve little accord, regardless of suddenly superior reported numbers. They are like a broken clock; they show the correct time twice a day but otherwise are dead wrong (and not to be bet on).

Manager Query: Which industry groups and which individual stocks were owned by you during each period, and how long had you owned these securities that produced your largest percentage gains in each period? Present a breakdown of your holdings as per Client Guide 6.

Beware of Managers Submitting Selective Periods of Performance to You—and Beware of Using "Magic Periods" in Performance Evaluation

One very dangerous approach to manager selection or retention is to concentrate on "magic periods" of time that are not reflective of investing realism. For example, there were many high-powered marketing efforts made in 1980 by managers sporting (and emphasizing) great 5-year equity performance records (1975 through 1979). While 5 years seems like a reasonable assessment time, the period of large gains from 1975 through 1979 had followed two disastrous stock market years (1973 and 1974). In most cases, those who prospered handsomely in 1975 and 1976 were the very managers and investors who were harshly treated in the 2 preceding years, and vice versa. Manager comparisons for this period show exactly this. This is the way it will be for those assessing 3- to 5-year performance numbers looking back from 1986. Concentration will be on 1983 through 1985 or on 1981 through 1985, omitting the very dynamic market of 1980. Compensating for this by skipping to a "magic" 10-year assessment will hardly solve the problem, since (again) the horrible 1973 and 1974 years will be excluded.

To guard against this, *you should: (1) go back as far as you can in assessing results (get as full a picture as you can); (2) make sure that particularly volatile years are included; and (3) assess manager size and all the potentially deceptive sources of performance emphasized in this chapter.*

Manager Query: Provide me with all-inclusive performance numbers for every cumulative period of your management over the past 10 or 15 years (e.g., 1-, 2-, 3-, 4-, 5-, 6-, 7-, 8-, 9-, 10-, 11-year cumulative results). Include any abnormalities, positive or negative, that affected any periods.

CONCLUSION

As ceaselessly repeated, performance statistics can be among the damnedest lies. You must dig deep to recognize the reasons for the reported figures. Although some managers may resist providing the information asked for in the Manager Queries, you do have a right to it—though it's one that few clients have yet insisted on. Without this probing, you are very likely to be deceived by numbers that are unrealistic, deceptive, and probably likely to move in an opposite direction.

8

MAKING BETTER
SENSE OF
BALANCED BOND
AND STOCK
ACCOUNTS

Managers assigned to invest in both bonds and stocks in one account naturally require more performance measurement than managers assigned only one asset. While the sum of the parts—the *total* portfolio result—is the most important consideration and is easily assessed by you, there is lots to be learned beyond this. You should know, for example, whether your manager's talents lie only in bonds, only in stocks, or mainly in the shifting between the two. If the firm under consideration is poor at any one of these talents, you should consider retaining it for its specialty and looking elsewhere for management of the weak suit.

The disturbing fact is that you probably get inadequate information to assess either your manager's strengths and weaknesses or (equally important) his faithfulness to your objectives. For example, here is how 90+ percent of balanced accounts are reported to clients for any given periods (only 1-year results are used for this illustration):

Asset	Market Value	Portion of Total	Total Return for the Year	Performance for the Year	Comparable Representative Performance Index for the Year
Cash	$ 4,000,000	40.0%	$ 400,000	+10.0%	None*
Bonds	3,000,000	30.0	(150,000)	− 5.0%	+ 1.0% (XYZ Bond Index)
Stocks	3,000,000	30.0	600,000	+20.0%	+15.0% (S&P 500 Index)
Total	$10,000,000	100.0%	$ 850,000	+ 8.5%	(to be discussed)

There are numerous problems with this format, most of which stem from your inability to determine where cash belongs. You know that cash constitutes 40 percent of your assets, but you don't know where it might be directed at any time; and you don't know where to credit its 10 percent return. In addition, the returns of −5 percent for bonds and +20

---

*Actually, clients should determine whether their cash reserves are earning what they should. For this illustration, however, no criterion has been assumed.

percent for stocks refer only to the 30 percent of your portfolio each represents.

In short, not only do you have an incomplete picture of your portfolio, but you also have a potentially deceptive picture.

There is a simple way to overcome these shortcomings, perhaps best explained by looking at two hypothetical accounts: one where the manager has been hired for equity investing and one where the assignment is to balance the account with bonds and stocks.

In the pure equity account, performance measurement and communication entail no more complications than those mentioned in past chapters. Bottom line returns can be compared against whatever equity index you choose; and any income from cash held in lieu of stocks is a part of the calculation. Your manager's choice is clear: If he retains cash, he does so in place of stocks. The choice is his, and the consequences of cash doing either better or worse than his invested stocks are "chargeable" to him. You should be cognizant of his cash either to determine how much risk has been taken (cash obviously being less risky than stocks) or to assess whether he is better at varying amounts of cash than at selecting stocks. Whatever your purpose, the calculation of returns from cash versus returns from invested stocks is easily figured and easily compared against any indices chosen. So performance for this account is uncomplicated and communication is clear.

By contrast, a balanced account with bond and stock assignments presents numerous problems. Whereas our pure equity illustration presented only two questions—those of risk and comparison to equity indices—your balanced account demands answers to the following additional questions:

1. How should relative performance of the total account be measured? What constitutes a representative comparison for the total portfolio?

2. How can you gauge how adept your manager has been in *each* of the two assets *if* cash has not been allocated specifically to either the bond or stock segments?

3. How can you judge risks taken in each asset *if* you don't know how much cash belongs to each?

4. Do you have to question your manager as to how he or she perceives your maximum or minimum potential invested positions in bonds or stocks at any time? How can you know whether your manager might have forgotten your stated objectives and might violate them at any time?

The solution starts with a discussion of the final point. Unless you choose to grant your manager free rein to move assets as desired, without limitations, you owe it to yourself and to your manager to match your goals and risk posture to some division of assets between stocks and bonds. The vast majority of client cases demand that some upper limit be set, generally between 50 and 80 percent for equity-type investments, with the residual in fixed-income (bond-type) holdings. Whatever ratio you and your manager set is *not* to be carved in stone. The relative values of bonds versus stocks will change, and your risk posture may change, too. Whatever you decide as a starting point, however, will *allow you to answer the four questions listed previously provided you insist that your manager set up separate pools for the potential investment of each of the*

STANDARD FORMAT

Asset	(1) Market Value	(2) Portion of Total	(3) Total Return for the Year	(4) Performance for the Year	(5) Comparable Representative Performance Index for the Year
Cash	$ 4,000,000	40.0%	$ 400,000	+10.0%	None
Bonds	3,000,000	30.0%	(150,000)	− 5.0%	+ 1.0% (XYZ Bond Index)
Stocks	3,000,000	30.0%	600,000	+20.0%	+15.0% (S&P 500 Index)
Total	$10,000,000	100.0%	$ 850,000	+ 8.5%	(to be discussed)

two assets. For example, if you have decided that a starting point of 60 percent in stocks is appropriate for you, insist that your manager set up this 60 percent for ultimate investment in equities (with 40 percent set aside for bonds). These 60 and 40 percent "pots" must carry their own segregated cash holdings, which *then create the equivalent of two pure accounts.* The equity pot is like the pure equity account described earlier; and the bond pot has the same reporting advantages.

You are now in a position to answer all of the four questions posed earlier, something that was impossible to do in today's widely used format. You will see this clearly by comparing the standard format (using the same figures shown at the beginning of this chapter) with what I call the Preferred Method. The following are repeats of this mythical portfolio both in today's standard format and in a less deceptive and far more informative and useful Client Guide 7.

Here are the specific advantages of the Preferred Method:

1. The division of your assets— 60 percent for potential investment in equities and 40 percent for bonds—is clear. If this is the ratio set by you, you can feel more confident that it will not be exceeded; if it has been set by your manager, you know his ultimate goals.

2. Your manager's degree of optimism for each asset is clear. You know that 25 percent of the bond "pot" is in cash, whereas 50 percent of the equity side is set aside in cash and uninvested in the chosen asset. Since strategy and responsibility have now been clearly defined, client/manager dialogue should be improved.

3. Risk assessment of each asset is more understandable, since the cash has been allocated to its potential "home."

4. Performance measurement has been simplified and improved. Here's how your analysis of returns will benefit:

   a. Your returns from cash are now properly allocated, so that your manager's choice either rewards or penalizes him within the separate bond and stock segments. In the fixed-income side, with cash allocated to its true home, this designated

CLIENT GUIDE 7
The Prefered Report for
Balanced Account Performance Measurement

	(1) Assets	(2) Portion of Total	(3) Total Return in Dollars	(4) Performance	(5) Representative Index
Fixed Income					
Invested bonds	$3,000,000	30%	$(150,000)	− 5.00%	
Cash set aside	1,000,000	10%	100,000	+10.00%	+1.0% performance of Shearson, Lehman/ Salomon Bros. combined indices
	$4,000,000	40%	$(50,000)	− 1.25%	
Equities					
Invested equities	$3,000,000	30%	$ 600,000	+20.0%	
Cash set aside	3,000,000	30%	300,000	+10.0%	
	$6,000,000	60%	$ 900,000	+15.0%	+15.0% performance of S&P 500
Total	$10,000,000	100%	$ 850,000	+ 8.5%	(to be discussed)

asset return was −1.25 percent compared with the +1.0 percent Shearson, Lehman/Salomon index—an unobtainable assessment in the standard report (which showed far more negative results of −5 percent for bonds—see line 2, column 4). Now look at equities: Stock selection (the invested portion of column 4) was a favorable +20 percent versus +15 percent for the S&P; but too much cash, definable where it belongs by the Preferred Method, brought total equity returns down to the same level as the S&P (line 6, column 4), again information clearly stated in the Client Guide but absent in the standard format. Hence a manager who in the standard format seemed to be significantly underperforming in fixed income is recognized as only slightly underperforming in the Preferred Method. At the same time, the manager's performance in stocks—which appeared superior in the standard report—is revealed as being only average using the Preferred report.

b.   You have overcome the very confusing and potentially deceptive performance calculations in the standard format on the *invested* portions of a portfolio. Reports that *only* measure invested portions show figures for "equities only" and "fixed income only"—which in our illustration amount to 75 percent of the fixed portion and 50 percent of potential equity exposure. The standard format, however, does not reflect the relative impact of those figures on the total portfolio. Carrying this to an admittedly ridiculous extreme, assume your manager owns only one stock and one bond. If the former doubles in price, the "equities only" figure would show +100 percent (plus dividend return), and this would normally be compared against whatever stock index has been chosen, or possibly though unfairly against other managers who may be fully invested in stocks. Whatever happens to the manager's one bond holding creates an equally deceptive number for comparative purposes.

Since reports of "equities only" or "fixed income only" segments too often either fail to highlight the percentage impact each is having on an account or are (generally) buried in the report, severe misinterpretations occur. Clients stare at figures that they believe to be significant but that may in fact be trivial or at least should be viewed differently.

Our firm has experienced this type of confusion innumerable times. In some cases, we have been praised for one asset capability and damned for another when in fact performance over the time period involved should have provoked the reverse response.

A consultant's report for the year 1983 to one of our clients produced just such confusion. The year had been a poor one for fixed-income securities (bond prices dropped as interest rate rose), while common stocks fared quite well. Our bond management group had correctly anticipated the interest rate surge, had sold off most longer-term bonds, had set aside some cash reserves and had shifted to shorter maturity bonds in their designated fixed-income portion of this client's balanced portfolio. We earned high income on these cash reserves and shorter-maturity bonds—enough to offset some losses incurred in the remaining invested bonds; our net result, using the Preferred presentation, showed a positive return of 5.6 percent for the year versus negative numbers for representative bond indices. Unfortunately, some moderate cash positions (10 to 20 percent) in the equity portion of this client's account had the opposite result on equity performance. We did indeed earn 12 percent on the cash set aside here, but the stock market rose about 22 percent for the year, so the cash was a drag. Our equity portion of the account, therefore, was up only 20 percent by our calculations.

The consultant's reported results to our client bore little resemblance to our figures. They ignored our segregated asset pots and had no way of allocating cash to either a bond or stock portion. Their system was oblivious to the fact that managers of any asset have a constant choice between owning that asset or holding cash. To them, cash belonged all by itself.

Without proper allocation of cash, the consultant's figures varied from ours as follows:

	Consultant	Ours (Preferred)
Bonds	−1.5%	+5.6%
Stocks	+22.5%	+20.5%

The consultant's figures ranked our firm in the bottom 25 percent of his bond manager sample and in the top 25 percent in stocks. This led to the following client remark: "You did fine in equities, but you certainly had a problem in fixed income." Their appraisal was exactly opposite from our true experience— something that we could refute fairly readily because we could admit that the conclusion was too favorable to us in one area while arguing that we were being unfairly judged in another. In other words, because our self-analysis seemed unbiased, it was easier for them to accept than if we were only arguing that we were being damned unnecessarily.

We, and other managers, face this frustration time and again in balanced accounts. Sometimes we look better than we should, sometimes worse. Sometimes the clients understand the problem, but most often they do not.

Again, since the total portfolio results are the same under both the standard and Preferred formats, is it really worth the bother to separate results as suggested?

If you are a "don't bother me with details, all I want is results" client, you will miss the importance. You will be looking at distortions, and these, along with lack of empathy and understanding, will only lead you to poor reasoning and potentially costly manager shifting. Nobody should oppose manager changes per se, but these decisions should be based on consistent and reliable information, not meaningless or deceptive figures.

HOW TO ASSESS *TOTAL* ACCOUNT PERFORMANCE

Both the standard and Preferred formats of Client Guide 7 show identical results of +8.5 percent for the total account. But how should you assess this +8.5 percent? Against what indices?

Certainly it is unfair to compare balanced results against either pure bond or stock indices. Since the definition of balanced account is "mixed assets," the performance standard should reflect the mix rather than any one of the parts.

The Preferred report allows exactly this: Maximum allotment to each asset is clearly delineated, enabling a ratio to be assigned for the total. For example, the 60−40 percent equities-to-bonds guideline evident from the Preferred report suggests that you assign a 60 percent weighting to your chosen equity standard (in this case, the S&P 500) and a 40 percent weighting to your bond index. Since the results for these two *indices* were +15 percent and +1.0 percent, respectively, the most efficient *total* account performance standard becomes:

$$
\begin{aligned}
\text{Equities } 60\% + 15.0\% &= +9.0\% \\
\text{Fixed} \quad\; 40\% + 1.0\% &= \underline{+0.4\%} \\
\text{Total} &\; +9.4\%
\end{aligned}
$$

Matching the actual total portfolio return of 8.5 percent to this 9.4 percent figure produces a sensible comparison, far better than what most managers and clients have to work with today.

It's worth repeating that asset mix portions are *not* to be carved in stone. Your objectives may be altered, just as manager recommendations may change. Varied results from bonds and stocks also demand attention: Strong performance from stocks and weak performance from bonds might soon change the 60 percent−40 percent ratio to, say, 70−30 percent, in which case the manager should shift sufficient equity money to fixed income to reestablish the 60:40 ratio.

In all cases, good communication between you and your manager is especially important in balanced accounts. Changes may or may not result, but whatever the changes in asset mix, you now have a method of comparing your manager fairly.

WHY HASN'T THE PREFERRED METHOD BEEN ADOPTED?

While the very consultants who compile today's confusing standard format are well aware of the problems it generates, they are hampered in any efforts to change by manager inability or unwillingness to provide better data.

The problem *can* be resolved, simply through consultant and client insistence that their managers set aside separate pools for potential equity and fixed-income investment. The result will be beneficial for everyone, as we have found any time adequate attention has been given by both client and consultant. The Preferred Method has clarified results and pinpointed where accolades and criticisms truly belong. However, it is not always easy to get all parties involved to agree on using the Preferred Method. After all, clients may have other managers who refuse to recognize the problem (they may not want to incur the expenses of new computer programs to accommodate such reporting); and consultants are torn between their desire to get decent data and their fear that their existing samples may be recognized as having less credibility.

The fact is that few managers have adequate records to enable them to alter their historical inputs to either clients or consultants. If managers haven't been delineating separate asset pots, if they themselves don't know to which segment cash has belonged, their hands are tied. For past years' performance, therefore, the focus may have to be on total fund performance, not on the parts. A better solution is to compare any manager's separate bond and stock pots (a la our Preferred Method) against a consultant's pure fixed income and pure equity samples. But this hardly diminishes the need for change from now on. As more managers convert to the Preferred bookkeeping and reporting, consultants and others who compile performance data will have larger and better samples to offer. Industry standards will rise, and clients will find it much easier to separate the wheat from the chaff of performance figures, especially in the muddle of balanced account results.

CONCLUSIONS

The Preferred Method of analyzing balanced account results accomplishes the following:

1. It forces clients to clarify objectives and to be more specific.
2. It forces managers to confirm their understanding of client objectives with specific asset allocations.

3. As markets change, it demands more clearly defined moves by either party.

4. It produces reports in more logical detail, allocating performance numbers where they should be.

5. It accurately points out manager strengths and weaknesses, allowing clients to assess whether managers are most proficient in managing any one asset type and allowing better assessment of manager ability to shift asset ratios.

6. It produces an efficient way to compare total portfolio results against an easy-to-understand standard.

Better and more precise communication, improved record keeping, and more reliable performance data are nondebatable goals for all clients. Until now, balanced accounts have been a special case, obstructing sound manager assessments. The Client Guide in this chapter, including, of course, the philosophies supporting it, should help you identify the best managerial talents to manage a variety of assets.

Of course, emphasis here has been on relative performance—certainly not the end-all for clients. As L. Guy Palmer, a former successful money manager now head of a portion of General Motors' pension effort, says: "You can't eat relative results." If you're doing well on a relative basis but losing absolute money, your comparative superiority does not produce the hard dollars necessary to pay ultimate responsibilities. Absolute returns are *the* crucial element over time, as are *real* (adjusted for inflation) results. In judging your manager's performance, the combination of all three— relative, absolute, and real returns—should be considered. One way to make consistent judgments when balanced accounts are involved is to follow the Client Guide and related procedures recommended in this chapter.

9

JUDGING THE RISKS TAKEN BY YOU OR YOUR MANAGER

Beauty is but skin-deep.
An old English proverb

Value is in the eyes of the beholder.
An equally old investment proverb

I once knew a broker who invested a huge amount of his clients' money in the stock of a company that was managed by people with shady reputations and had a weak income and financial position disguised by flimsy, dishonest accounting. The stock went up for some unknown reason, however, and the broker sold his holdings for a big gain. He boasted of his brilliance to everyone within earshot. One day he was bragging to a small group when someone informed him that the company had just filed for bankruptcy—a brief 3 months after he had made his coup.

"Don't you think you should temper your statements now?" suggested one of the group. "It's clear that you risked your clients' funds beyond their understanding or desires."

"Wrong," replied the broker. "It's the result that counts."

"Well," snapped the broker's critic, "I don't reward the boatman who takes me down the river in a vessel that, unbeknownst to me, has a leaky bottom. I deserve to be apprised of risks taken on my behalf. And my respect is highest for those who have my total welfare at heart. You, my friend, are a leaky-bottom investor, and somebody ought to take your 'paddle' away!"

Indeed, risk has been, is, and always will be the "flip side" of rate of return—to be seriously appraised by every investor or client before, during, and after success is measured. It is critical to practically every investment decision, ranging from:

Knowing your investor self and setting investment objectives

Making investments yourself

Choosing the right manager if you are going to entrust money to others

Assessing your own results or the results of those hired to manage your funds

Because risk is so integral to all aspects of investing, it has been referred to directly and indirectly throughout the preceding pages. But now it is time to isolate and analyze risk—to help you judge how much money you might reasonably expect to make or lose with different managers and to help you separate out deserved performance accolades from undeserved ones.

MEASURING RISK

The trouble with discussing risk is that it is so difficult to measure. The literal definition is clear: All dictionaries define risk as an exposure to chance of loss. Investment practitioners often state it somewhat differently, defining risk to include the uncertainties surrounding *expected* returns.

The gap between broad definition and efficient measurement, however, is very wide. In practice, both "exposure to loss" and "uncertainties surrounding future returns" are highly amorphous considerations. Except in the case of Treasury bills and their equivalents (which offer minimal risk of loss and maximal certainty of return, but which carry the risks of lost opportunity or of diminishing purchasing power), risk determination is *very* imprecise. The only certainties in risk assessment are:

1.   Subjectivity is *always* involved, which of course only ensures that risk management will *never* be precise.

2.   Even the best statistical representations of risk are to be questioned. Samples are never all-inclusive, but even if they were, the fact that conditions change and that the future seldom directly parallels the past make the conclusions from all but the best of work suspect.

3.   Perception of risk depends on the "filter" of those involved. For clients, perception will differ based on each investor's financial position and investing personality—which combine to produce responses to interim fluctuations in price and eventual gains and losses. For managers, risk perception differs according to self-image; that is, the more confident managers are, the more they believe they can control their destinies—and the less sensitive they are to possible errors.

4.   Time is a factor, too. In assessing a loss, it is very possible that one has simply not allowed sufficient time for the investment to blossom.

Just as value *is* in the eyes of the beholder, perception of risk varies from client to client, from manager to manager, and from circumstance to circumstance. Most investors agree that risk and return should correspond to one another, but the philosophies, egos, fantasies, and personality traits of most managers lead them to believe they can achieve more of one side of the equation (profits) without a comparable expense or exposure of the other side (risk). "That," as they say, "is what makes horse racing (and investing)!" And that is what makes it difficult for clients, who simply have to accept the following fact of life: *You cannot expect managers to admit that large losses were "deserved" or that they may be incurred in the future.*

The onus is on you, therefore, to be skeptical of what you are told about risk taken with your funds. You had better form your own opinions of it, both to protect yourself against surprises and to improve your investing through others.

IMPROVING YOUR RISK ASSESSMENT CAPABILITIES

Needless to say, mountains of work have been written on the delicate subject of risk. The approach here is not to solve the age-old problem of correct definition (since there is no one correct definition), but instead to simplify risk assessment so that you can make more intelligent judgments and improve communication with anyone who helps you with your investing.

FUNDAMENTAL FACTORS

Prior to the advent of modern portfolio theory (MPT), risk assessment concentrated solely on so-called fundamental factors, which included:

1.   Making equity risk judgments based on the basic business and the company represented by the security being considered—that is, assessing the potential vulnerability of the industry and the company to negative fluctuations in earnings or dividends.

2.   Relating the market price of the security to net income, cash flow, dividends, or book value per share—with the least premium paid for such fundamental factors signifying the least amount of risk.

3. Supplementing the standard fundamentals with others designed to signify company qualities, including: returns earned on company assets and accumulated equity; past volatility (standard deviation) of past earnings; and strength of financial position and balance sheets.

Behind these judgments lay other related factors, such as a company's size, its foreign exposure, its currency risks, accounting practices, and management capabilities, plus considerations such as marketability of the security, its popularity, the dispersion of (security) analysts' forecasts, and so on.

Most investors consider most of these factors, *paying special attention to trends in the future.* As meticulous as one might be in correlating market price to many of these considerations, conclusions will be meaningless if the future is to change radically. Hence the high degree of subjectivity mentioned means that *approximation* of risk is the best that one can strive for.

MPT's INFLUENCE ON RISK ASSESSMENT

The development of MPT expanded the study of risk considerably. With the aid of the computer, numerous talented people traced history, made correlations, and developed a language all their own to quantify risk. There was major concentration on the relative market price volatility of stocks, a factor that MPT proponents termed *beta*, but some even more complicated proxies for risk (alphas, R^2's, standard deviations, variances, covariances) also surfaced to compete with traditional, fundamental risk measures. A very brief glossary of terms you are most likely to encounter would include the following—all related to a total portfolio of stocks:

Beta. The linchpin of MPT. It is derived from past volatility relative to the market (the S&P 500), with 1.00 signifying duplication of the market. A 1.10 beta indicates that volatility in price has been 10 percent greater than the market, and MPTers would therefore claim that portfolio performance results ought to be at least 10 percent greater than the market, too. Most MPTers measure risk by beta calculations, the higher the beta meaning the higher the risk, and vice versa. They contend that clients should make risk/return assessments based on either past or projected beta numbers.

Specific Risk. Attempts to measure volatility unrelated to the market—that is, based instead on characteristics of the company—whereas beta is a measure of risk derived from the upward or downward movement of the general market. The average stock's price volatility unexplained by the overall market has been about 20 to 25 percent, according to MPTers.

Alpha. The investment return that arises from taking nonmarket (specific) risk. Alpha attempts to measure how well a manager selects stocks that are undervalued. The higher the alpha, the better the selection. (Anything over 1.5 percent per year above the market is considered very good.)

R^2. Quantifies how closely a stock or portfolio's performance has replicated the market. R^2 for an individual stock is typically quite low (0.2 or 0.3), but a portfolio holding 20 to 30 stocks tends to cancel out many of the specific factors. Therefore, portfolio R^2 will tend to be much higher than 0.3. R^2 is used to measure diversification of portfolio relative to the market, with 1.00 being equal to the market (an index fund). If you have hired a manager to be "active" and have faith in his judgment, you should expect a low R^2 (anything below about 0.95).

To say that the new risk proxies created a wide schism in the investment community is an understatement. Traditionalists railed at the suggested exactness of beta and other measures. They were either overwhelmed by or suspicious of the higher mathematics, and they were skeptical of the selection and back-testing of data involved. They found even more to criticize with the MPT emphasis on *relative market volatility* (relative to the S&P 500) *as a proxy for risk.*

While some traditionalists quarreled about all aspects of beta, most accepted the measure as reasonably sensible so long as the volatility judged was *in sync with the market.* For example, a stock (or a portfolio of stocks) that consistently increased 10 percent more than an up market and decreased 10 percent more than a down market over a series of market cycles, producing a beta of 1.1, was indeed more volatile than one that increased 10 percent less than an up market and decreased 10 percent less than a down market (a beta of 0.9). Serious questioning erupted, however, with the calculation of "negative" betas for stocks or portfolios that behaved in totally opposite ways to the market—for example, those that were generally falling throughout a prolonged rising market. The critics legitimately cried: "Are such stocks really less risky, as negative betas suggest?" MPTers explained that investors should avoid reading too much into the beta measurement alone. The negative beta example, they explained, represents those rare exceptions where the direction of the stock market had essentially no impact on the individual security.* Despite this explanation, many investors were skeptical of a system that produced any integral numbers that belied a practical investment sense.

In addition, many skeptics took heart from the opinions of some of the world's most formidable investors, such as Warren Duffet, and heralded investment experts, such as the late Benjamin Graham, who calmly but forcefully argued that beta constituted a poor substitute for risk analysis. Their criticism emanated from the belief that, even if beta were a good measure of past relative volatility, it was not necessarily a good predictor of future volatility. Most important, neither Buffet or Graham was concerned with short-term market fluctuations. Their definition of risk centered on the probability of any company's being unable to meet investor expectations for growth in earnings, dividends, or book value over time—fundamentals not considered in beta calculations.

The MPTers countered by arguing that individual stocks may be inconsistent in market risk analysis, but the combined betas of numerous securities even out the inconsistencies—that is, beta explains over 90 percent of the performance of most *portfolios* as opposed to only 20 to 30 percent for the average individual stock. The MPTers contended further that they could supply numerical gauges that fundamental analyses could not. After all, no one ratio of fundamental factors had yet proven to be a

---

*In technical terms, a regression R^2 of close to zero.

reliable risk measure. Say what you like about strong balance sheets, steady growth, low price/earnings ratios, or understated assets—the bugaboo of subjectivity reduced confidence in the resulting measure.

Like all risk analysis, beta has its times of apparent effectiveness and times of very poor relationships. In 1984, for example, portfolio betas were poor predictors of performance. That year, the S&P produced total returns of 6.1 percent—yet the highest results came from the lowest betas. As Wayne Wagner of the consulting firm Wilshire Associates stated: "Capital market theory was a big failure in 1984."

Time has healed much of the fundamentals versus beta controversy. Many of the original advocates of beta became disenchanted with its use. Others, such as Dr. William Sharpe of Stanford's Graduate School of Business and Dr. Barr Rosenberg of the University of California (Berkeley) Business School, presented provocative adjustments to historic betas—adjustments that combined numerous fundamental considerations to accomplish what all investors strive for: predicting future risk. *Value Line*, one of the better investment statistical services, now combines elements of MPT with past and projected fundamental factors to arrive at its risk proxies.

Some merging of thought was inevitable. It would have been myopic for even the staunchest supporters of the fundamental approach to risk to dismiss beta altogether. After all, if the fundamental factors require subjectivity, why not at least include other factors that require similar subjectivity? As for MPT, not only is its efficiency open to question, but many of its measures tend, in the vast majority of cases, to confuse more than they enlighten.

A personal experience in 1981 suggests that a myriad of complicated statistical approaches can lead to more problems than they might solve. The occasion was a client meeting attended by two representatives of our firm, eight client committee members, and two consultants. We had just completed a highly successful year in 1980, owing in large part to two industry group holdings: oil/oil service and technology. We were prepared to talk about the above-average risks we perceived in the two groups, something that had caused us to commence selling significant portions of both. One of the consultants volunteered to discuss his risk analysis, which oddly enough did not indicate that the oils were the least bit risky. His approach was based on betas and on other measures that would have challenged a cum laude math or statistics major. Only two client representatives had the slightest understanding of the terminology used, and, frankly, we weren't much more knowledgeable.

The result was 45 minutes of confusion, those assembled resembling three different language groups trying to converse without an interpreter. In this case, the consultant's interpretation of our risk posture was more conservative than ours—which made our selling position appear foolish to our clients. Had the disagreement been over holding securities that the consultant considered far riskier than we did, the meeting would have been even more difficult.

Disagreement over risk in terms that *can be understood* by clients is a healthy exercise. Disagreement accompanied by confusion is mainly destructive. To expect many trustees, directors, committee members, or individuals to comprehend the meanings of esoteric statistical terms and to interpret them wisely is unrealistic.

WHAT TO DO ABOUT RISK ASSESSMENT

Both fundamental and MPT type investors agree on one principle—that *managers and clients should assess risk on the basis of a total list of securities.* As Professor John G. McDonald of Stanford's Graduate School of Business says, "You don't judge risk either by the strongest or weakest link." Indeed, investors should know how all their "trees" fit into their "forest."

How can managers express this to you, the client? How can you assess whether their returns were achieved because they gambled heavily or, instead, whether they were achieved through low risk exposure? Likewise, what clues exist to future performance?

A good beginning is to ascertain whether managers can explain their investment selections to your satisfaction. They should be able to communicate where *their* perception of value exists, whether it be some ratio of price to earnings, book value, yield, working capital per share, popularity, volatility, and so on. A manager's style should show through in this analysis; it should be clear to you whether he sticks to risks with which he is apparently knowledgeable and comfortable as opposed to approaches that have been foreign to him or that you have dictated against in your objectives. Style consistency can be meangingful to managerial assessment.

You should also watch for all sorts of extremes—for large holdings of securities with, for example, the following characteristics:

1. High P/E's, especially in relation to *realistic* growth or versus historical relative multiples.

2. Companies burdened with highly leveraged balance sheets—with heavy debt in relation to equity. (Just as an investor's risk increases as he borrows, leveraged companies normally subject their owners to greater risk.)

3. Concentration of money in a few industry groups. (The manager who has plunked your money into five or six industries has placed your eggs into a small number of baskets—and if those "eggs" are historically volatile, leveraged groups, such as airlines, autos, steels, and the like, you better believe the risk is high.)

Number of securities held is another consideration. The ridiculous example of owning one security only, with its commensurate exposure to wide price swings, is obvious. In between a single holding and 60 to 70 is a wide gap; while there are drawbacks in holding many, many issues, which tends to foster mediocrity,* degree of concentration is a risk consideration. The standard number of securities in a portfolio normally varies according to the capital invested and the type of securities owned. For assets between $500,000 and $50 or $100 million, holdings will generally

---

*Some managers prosper handsomely despite owning numerous securities. Capital Research, John Templeton (Templeton Funds), and others have hardly suffered despite owning long lists of stocks. *There is a big difference between investors who diversify widely in company ownership but who make significant industry or other strategic bets and managers who seem to own everything or who are so scattered that supervision of portfolio is difficult.*

range from a low of 10 to 15 in the smaller-size portfolios to a high of 60 to 70 or even higher in elephant-size accounts.

Industry and company risks, of course, constantly change. What looks secure today may be vulnerable tomorrow, and vice versa. Indeed, there is a school of thought that points to a stock's *popularity* as the greatest risk of all. Too much popularity equals too much demand equals inflated price is a truism that describes high risk as well as any. The corollary to this is that lack of investor acceptance lowers risk substantially. But there are extremes to beware of here, too; for instance, a portfolio containing only the most unpopular stocks is bound to represent mostly unattractive companies operating in mainly unattractive industries. The holdings may be unpopular for good reasons—that is, they may represent cyclical, highly leveraged industries that suffer from inferior secular trends, or they may represent companies slated soon to experience disappointing results. Thus, a manager who owns only very unpopular securities may be exposing clients to high risk regardless of investor disenchantment. The expression "If you sleep with dogs, you are likely to get fleas" is not to be dismissed. As with very broad ownership of securities, however, there are managers who specialize in owning "inferior" companies and who have profited from doing so.

It's worth emphasizing again how risky it is to follow others in very popular trends. It may feel comfortable to huddle along with other investors, but the historical evidence is clear: Such conformity implies that high prices are being paid and that danger lies ahead.

WHAT ABOUT CASH AS A RISK OFFSET?

The tactic of holding cash to counterbalance high-risk investing is sensible. But cash and its derivative investment style of market timing are not always as riskless as they appear. High transaction and execution costs, along with the difficulties of judging the big market moves, have combined to produce below-average results for most timers. Studies have overwhelmingly proved that good company or industry selection has been more productive than frequently playing general market swings. Of course, the topic here is risk, not returns. Describing market timing differently, if you guess incorrectly and are fully invested when the market is falling but are lightly invested when the trend is up, large capital loss risk exists.

In a way, the insistence by many market timers that their style entails low risk is similar to claims made by certain managers who practice a limitation of loss strategy to each purchase. It may sound reassuring (low risk) to hear that any security that drops some given percentage is automatically liquidated. But where does the money go from there? If it is slated to flow into another security that then declines in price, where is the protection? Obviously, the only protection is against a big loss in any single security, not against large declines in total assets. The bottom line is obviously far more meaningful than fragments of a theory.

BACK TO FINAL RISK ASSESSMENT

So there are theories, often ballyhooed by managers in marketing presentations and client meetings, that sound like clear assessments of risk but are not. Intelligent risk assessment, therefore, demands three S's: skepticism, sensibleness, and sophistication. And it cries for regular, mature, and understandable communication between your manager and you.

Sensible communication must force an investment portfolio to reveal its risk nature. Since both the MPT and fundamentalist camps agree that risk should be judged by a look at the total portfolio rather than a focus on its isolated parts, you would think that clients have been receiving such information. While some consultants and certain managers do this, too many do not; those who do too often present an incomplete picture.

Client Guides 8 and 8a illustrate how risk can be measured *and understood*. Pertinent information has been added to today's standard formats, which normally present individual common stock holdings by industry weightings and which sort fixed-income portfolios by type of issuers (governments, utilities, corporates or municipalities). Important characteristics of the separate holdings have been added—and these have then been factored according to their proportionate weightings within the portfolio. *The result is a portfolio presented as if it were an individual security*—an ideal starting point for an intelligent discussion of risk and its all-important fit with your objectives.

The following are two illustrations of the Guide. The first (Client Guide 8) depicts how a bond portfolio should be viewed. Lots of pertinent information is presented, including a summary of the total portfolio's characteristics on the very bottom line. Columns (7) through (13) should be very meaningful to any client trying to assess the inherent values and approximate risks of his holdings. To illustrate, let's assume this summary is presented to you in August of 1986. Column (7) concludes that your average bond matures on July 6, 1992—slightly less than 6 years from now; this intermediate-term maturity date is certainly less risky than, say, a 20-year average maturity. Column (8)'s yield to maturity of 10.9 percent can now be compared with other 6-year maturity bonds available in the marketplace. Columns (9) and (10) show Moody's top rating of "AAA" plus the manager's own risk rating of 90 (on a 100 scale); and (11) summarizes another manager input, this one on marketability of the securities (8 on a scale of 10). Column (12) is the so-called "duration" of the portfolio—a time measure similar to average maturity, intended to depict potential *price volatility*. The duration number attempts to predict how much price change will follow each 1 percent of interest rate change—i.e., the Guide's total of a 5.7 duration suggests that each 1 percent move in rates will cause a 5.7% move in market price. The duration number can be compared with any market index chosen by the client as his performance standard, providing a practical gauge of price risk being taken by the manager. Finally, the three segments of (13) present the manager's view of his own risk/return formula—not important to detail here, but another input that, combined with the others, provides a total view to which every client is entitled but that is normally sadly lacking. Omitting the manager's projections, the presentation provides a basis for much-improved performance measurement and risk assessment. You have an understandable picture of your portfolio—by maturity, quality, and marketability—that you can judge against your risk-taking standards. And, assuming that the conclusions reflect your manager's portfolio structure in prior periods, you can relate your account's results to an intelligent standard.

CLIENT GUIDE 8
Fixed-Income Portfolio[a]

	(1) Par Value (000's)	(2) Market Value (000's)	(3) Percentage of Total	(4) Average Coupon	(5) Average Current Return	(6) Average Price	(7) Average Maturity	(8) Average Yield to Maturity	(9) Moody's Rating	(10) Mgr. Credit Rating	(11) Marketability Rating	(12) Duration	(13) Average Estimated Rates of Return ESP	OPT	RISK
Cash Equivalents	18,500	18,500	22	8.5	8.5	100.00	12/30/86	8.5	AAA	100	10	0	8.0	7.0	9.7
U.S. government and government guaranteed obligations	43,000	45,700	56	12.2	11.3	108.38	11/30/95	10.8	AAA	100	9	8.0	11.0	13.0	6.5
Mortgage pass-throughs	16,000	16,500	21	10.1	11.0	92.7	12/15/92	12.1	AAA	95	7	4.5	13.2	14.5	9.5
Other Sectors:															
Industrial	—														
Finance & banking	—														
Foreign – Canadian	—														
Total portfolio	77,500	81,250	100	10.9	10.6	103.9	07/06/92	10.9	AAA	90	8	5.7	11.8	13.1	8.5

[a]Total rates of return forecast for the period ending June 30, 1986.
Reinvestment interest rate assumption: 8.8%.

CLIENT GUIDE 8a
A Sensible Way To View an Equity Portfolio

	Account	S&P 500	
Company Sales and Net Income Figures:			
Past 5 years, growth (per year):			
Sales	12.0%	7.2%	Companies owned in the account have
Earnings per share	14.0	6.1	grown 50-110% faster than the S&P.
Cash flow per share	16.0	8.0	
Dividends per share	12.0	8.0	
Past 5 years, average:			Managements of companies owned have
Return on assets	19.0	12.0	achieved higher returns than the average
Return on equity	22.0	17.0	(S&P) company.
Past 10 years:			
Volatility of earnings			Less fluctuation in profits from the
(Standard deviation of earnings per share)	22.0	32.0	portfolio companies vs. the S&P.
Financial position (latest year):			Portfolio co's have less debt and higher
Debt/capital ratio	20.0	32.0	balance sheet qualities.
S&P quality rating	A	A-	
Past market volatility (beta)	1.05	1.00	Holdings 5% more volatile than S&P.
Portfolio diversification (R^2)	0.75	1.00	Manager is making strategic bets - not simply duplicating the market.

133

	Account	S&P 500
Company Sales and Net Income Figures:		
Current market price information:		
Current yield	3.0	4.2
P/E on latest 12 months	13.0	11.0
P/cash flow, latest 12 months	9.0	7.5
Price to book value	2.8	2.0
Average market capitalization	7.0 billion	11.0B.
Other:		
Reinvestment rate[a]	14.7%	10.0%
Manager projections:		
3–5-year growth rate	14.0%	9.0%
Earnings per share growth, next 12 months	+13.0%	+5.5%
Current P/E on earnings per share, next 12 months	11.5x	10.5x
Portfolio characteristics:		
Growth stocks	60.0%	30%
Growth/cyclical stocks	20.0%	30%
Cyclical stocks	10.0%	20%
Defensive stocks	5.0%	15%
Other stocks	5.0%	5%

Handwritten notes:
- Portfolio income 1.2%/year less than S+P.
- Premium price of 15-20% for the portfolio vs. the market.
- Portfolio priced high relative to book value.
- Your own smaller cos than the S+P—but still very large ones on average.
- Manager projections are in line with past experience.
- If EPS projections are accurate, the premium being paid is less than 10% over the S+P P/E in exchange for 50-100% more projected growth. Sounds like reasonable value growth for your portfolio.
- Manager's style is apparently one that concentrates on growth stocks. You should have known this —and this summary should confirm it.

[a]Used by many security analysts to "prove" the likelihood of future growth rates. Calculation is: return on equity (in this case 22.0%) times retained (not shown, but if the average company in this portfolio paid out 33% of EPS, the retained portion of 67% multiplied by the 22.0% return on equity equals 14.7%, slightly above the 14.0% average for the past 5 years and the 14.0% being projected by the manager for the next 3 to 5 years).

Now see how much more interesting—and informative—a portfolio of common stocks can be. You will find many more fundamental filters than MPT numbers in Client Guide 8a, simply because there *are* more fundamental inputs readily available to most clients and because these are more understandable to most. (One of the advantages of the fundamental approach is that it parallels the business or investment training of individuals.)

For comparison purposes, the summary figures for the account have been placed alongside the same statistics for the S&P 500 Stock Index. My handwritten comments in the right-hand margin suggest how you might judge the account's characteristics, your manager's strategies and investment style, and the approximate risk being assumed.

It is easy to see in the Client Guide 8a example that the manager is holding securities with lower dividend yields and higher price/earnings and price/book value ratios, which he must be able to justify to you. In this case, he can point to superior past growth of sales, earnings, cash flow, dividends, and return on assets and equity of the companies held, as he can to lower volatility of earnings and to stronger balance sheet ratios and quality ratings. He has also provided projections so that you can assess the potential values inherent in your account. For example, if he is correct in his earnings outlook for the next 12 months (admitted a big "if"), the premiums paid to own the stocks may be very small relative to the portfolio's fundamental characteristics.

Although subjective judgments are still required, intelligent discussion between the manager and you should evolve, all aimed at a sensible assessment of risk and a determination that your objectives are being followed.

A final important use of Client Guides 8 and 8a is to gain a better understanding of performance results. Chapter 5 discussed the inevitability of investment cycles and the existence of manager investment styles. If you are to benefit from these cycles and styles, you must be able to identify which managers have already suffered or prospered from which past trends. The Client Guides paint a good picture of exposure to cycles and style. Client Guide 8a's portfolio, for example, should not have been expected to benefit from a market that neglected higher-growth, higher-P/E stocks, nor should it have been expected to prosper from a surge in small-capitalization companies (since the portfolio had an average market capitalization of $7.0 billion). If and when larger-growth companies return to investment vogue, the client should expect strong performance.

It is crucial for you to determine that the style you are getting is what you hired, just as it is crucial to make judgments of value and to understand why performance has been as it has. Your actions can become far more rational and well timed through the knowledge gained from following these examples, along with the recommendations on how to understand and benefit from cycles and styles discussed in Chapter 5.

CONCLUSIONS

Clients and managers need to work harder at risk assessment and should strive particularly to view risk through similar filters. Portfolios should become more like pointillistic paintings, where the "dots" (the individual securities held) are secondary to the total "picture" (the characteristics of the total portfolio). Client Guides 8 and 8a may not produce the beauty of the pointillistic works of Seurat or Signac, but they provide the framework for a practical understanding of risk and an essential link between performance results and sound manager assessment.

> *Manager Query:* *Provide your assessment of risk in an understandable and specific manner. Show me my portfolio* as if it represented one holding and relate this to your past managerial style and beliefs.*

---

*Or, if this is not your present manager, *"a composite of all existing manager accounts with similar objectives to mine."*

10

CHOOSING THE INVESTMENT MANAGER WINNERS: DEFINING A MANAGER'S PHILOSOPHY AND ASSESSING MANAGEMENT PERSONNEL

It may be that the race is not always to the swift; nor the battle to the strong. But that's the way to bet!

Damon Runyon

Prospective clients should view investment managers like icebergs: To avoid danger, clients should examine their submerged qualities as meticulously as their most visible attribute—their performance record. Actually, the hidden qualities may demand far more attention! Even Dean LeBaron, whose Batterymarch Financial has amassed a fine long-term performance record, states unequivocally: "Performance figures are worthless; they have zero predictive value."

Although there are hundreds of billions of dollars under professional management, at fees amounting to hundreds of millions, very little of substance is known of the people or the organizations entrusted with these huge investment responsibilities. As stated, performance assessment has, up to now, created confusion; the process of assessing quality has left much to be desired. Clients often exert more effort in hiring a few clerks than they do in choosing an investment manager to handle such important funds as pension and profit-sharing, endowment, foundation, savings, and large individual assets. Many decisions involving huge sums are made based on 45- to 60-minute interviews, with the majority of time allowed for manager-prepared presentation and a minimum for intelligent questioning by the prospective client.

A dramatic personal example comes to mind. I was a board member of a local charitable organization that was seeking investment management help. Appointments were made to interview four managers. One of the four made a particularly smooth and exciting presentation, the heart of which was an intricate internal system of security evaluations that was apparently responsible for much of the firm's performance record. After the presentation, the board practically gave a standing ovation to the manager; the money was certain to be awarded to him.

The fly in the ointment was that a key person from this organization had come to my office that very morning. A serious investor himself, and a person of high integrity, he had a dilemma: His organization was taking on many new accounts, but he was frustrated because his senior partner was devoting less and less time to the business (living away from his business home 4 to 6 months a year) and because their computer program was, in his words, "a shambles." He had made up his mind to leave his firm because of these "ethical" considerations.

Some lines of manager questioning—which I will detail later in this chapter—might well have enabled the board to uncover this lack of attention by one of the firm's key individuals. What would have been very hard to uncover was the problem with the firm's computer, which signaled that the presentation was exaggerated (if not dishonest). If coincidence had not dropped the information in our laps, the board would have rewarded what was froth and overstatement.

The case may be extreme, but shades of such experiences occur frequently in the awarding of money to managers. Actually, *a well-planned meeting, which includes intelligent questioning of decision-making systems at the manager firms' offices, is a "must" for prospective clients*. (It might have uncovered the phony computer system just as it might have revealed inadequate attention of key people.)

So the burden is on you to dig deeper than surface presentations to find the manager winners of the future. Sound qualitative efforts must be combined with your realistic probing of quantitative information. More inner sanctum unveilings of the investment management business will help a lot here. Just as the quantitative has its seamy side, the qualitative is shielded by many "bells and whistles" that tend to dazzle or confuse newcomers (and even many of the initiated).

This is not to imply that managers operate without legitimate systems, nor is it to suggest that all, or even most, participants are dishonest. There are, however some clever dog and pony shows out there—and it is easy, even for sophisticated clients, to be fooled.

What needs to be done? Shouldn't you raise your probabilities of separating the sound and practical approaches to great investment results from the "flaky" ones? Shouldn't you know enough to discern whether what you see in a manager is what you are destined to get?

Clients should adopt the approach of physicist Jacob Bronowski, as related to us by Studs Terkel in his memoir *Talking to Myself*. Bronowski once told Terkel, "Until you ask an impertinent question of nature, you do not get a pertinent answer. Great answers in nature are always hidden in the questions."

You have to ask impertinent questions if you are to separate out the superior from the inferior investment managers. Impertinent in this case does not mean rude or nasty; it means fresh and bold and unconventional. In other words, you must be willing—and prepared—to ask hard questions.

Recommended questioning will not be as esoteric as one of Bronowski's examples, of Einstein's doubting the long-held assumption that time is a given and then asking whether "my time is the same as yours?" Like Einstein, however, you can think differently from others. Instead of contributing to mathematics and science, the right impertinent questions can produce a theory of relativity of investment managers—and help you decide which managers are most likely to be the best from this point on. This chapter, as well as Chapters 11, 13, and 14, will show you how to achieve this by asking managers, in provocative ways, "How can you prove to me that your future is likely to be very positive, better than others, and perhaps even better than your past?"

Seven approaches have been developed to help you probe beyond the performance statistics and the surface appearances of investment managers. The first four (two here and two in Chapter 11) are useful both before and after the hiring decision has been made; they can help you choose the "right" manager and make intelligent assessments of how your account is then being managed. The final three involve specific tracking of manager actions and can be best undertaken by existing clients. These three, most useful in rethinking whether your original hiring decision was sound, will be outlined in Chapters 13 and 14. It may seem unnecessary, but it is probably worthwhile to remind you that *you* should be in control of any kind of manager assessment. The money is yours, and you are the one doing the hiring. Do *not* be intimidated by individuals, reputations, numbers of people, computer models, or fancy slide shows.

Your control of the process demands maintaining a consistency and fairness in your interviewing. Give all your prospects an even break. Do not follow the lead of one pension overseer I encountered. Our firm was one of two being considered for equity management of this individual's pension assets. Two meetings were scheduled, one for our firm at this individual's hotel and one at a competitor's office. Although we favored a meeting at our home base, too, where we could go on line with computer screens and introduce a number of our decision makers, we at least anticipated a quiet setting at the hotel.

When we arrived for our 8:30 A.M. appointment, we were informed that we would not meet in a private room but in the coffee shop. The potential client hadn't had breakfast yet, and the next hour or so was spent with as much attention to ordering and shuffling the French toast and coffee as to our investment process. (The coup de grace occurred when the maple syrup spilled on our papers!) Needless to say, concentration on the task at hand was hardly what it should have been. Managers cannot expect success with everyone, so they have to be understanding losers— but they do deserve equal time and presentation conditions.

FOUR APPROACHES TO MANAGER ASSESSMENT BEFORE *AND* AFTER THE HIRING DECISION HAS BEEN MADE

Defining a Manager's Investment Philosophy—and Determining Whether It Reflects Investment Realism

While some managers adhere to very rigid investment philosophies, owning securities with very specific criteria, you should not expect precision from every manager. But, with or without a rigid style, managers should be able to communicate some specific investment preferences. If they cannot, you will never fully understand what should and should not be expected from their management.

You should, for example, understand why a manager favors certain types of securities, and you should be able to visualize what your portfolio is likely to resemble. As a matter of fact, as intimated in Chapter 9 on risk, it is perfectly proper to ask to see certain of a manager's actual portfolios of stock and bond holdings. The best samples will be those of similar size, nature, and risk posture to yours. And the most instructive will be those showing the characteristics of Client Guides 8 and 8a. A manager's response to Client Guide 2a should be equally informative.

Defining manager style helps you understand what is to be expected from differing economic and stock market conditions. If Smokestack America prospers, leading to a surge in cyclical stocks, you should know which managers are likely and unlikely to profit. (Those investors who favor lower P/E's should benefit, whereas those who emphasize strong secular growth companies will participate less in the trend.) If, instead, the economy grows moderately and companies with exceptional unit demand prevail, the typical cyclical stock owner will normally underperform while the growth stock investor will enjoy superior results.

You certainly should understand the likely (not guaranteed) experience to be anticipated in rapidly rising or declining markets. The manager who promises exceptional results during ebullient times is implying that he is willing to assume high risks—which augurs for poor results in weak markets. Some may accomplish great returns without inordinate risk taking, but this accomplishment is decidedly the exception. As already discussed, however, *risk* is an elusive term open to many interpretations, so caution is advised regarding those who promise a utopia of high returns without high risk.

The avowed risk-averse manager is telling you that he expects to lag in bonanza periods but to excel, on a relative basis, in the worst periods. Again, a manager's philosophy itself—even supported by the past record—does not guarantee future results. This is especially true over a short time span. Like the consistent .333 hitter, it is the season that counts, not the first game.

Be especially wary of managers who imply unusual success or who imply precision in their approach, particularly those who promise unusual success along with very low risk. One publicity-conscious manager is known for his computerized stock selection system that practically guarantees a client limited downside (with, of course, maximum upside!). Under close analysis, however, his system relies almost exclusively on a stock's price relative to its net income over the preceding 12 months—a sensible approach so long as no major economic downturns are in store. If earnings are slated to drop sharply, his risks are far greater than he paints them to be. Thus it's not that his system cannot prove profitable, it's only that surprises are much more possible than he makes them out to be.

Every investment style has its risks. Moreover, markets are seldom identical to past patterns. Be very skeptical of those who claim to be able to call *short*-term swings in any financial market—an inconsistent and generally unsuccessful tack taken in both bonds and stocks over the years. Clients may have difficulty recognizing a prospective manager's low-probability claims such as these, because managers embracing such strategies seldom come right out and profess to be active traders. Regardless of the rhetoric, managers who pride themselves on extensive use of cash are admitting that an in-and-out market approach is a major weapon in their arsenal. If you have chosen such a manager, be forewarned that your portfolio will incur significant trading costs (brokerage commissions, custodian charges, possible tax burdens); understand also that your portfolio may hold large cash balances during intervals when the market is rising. Expect times when your hoped-for solid hitter has struck out while most other managers are garnering base hits.

Your expectations of a market timer should differ sharply from those of a manager espousing a philosophy of being fully invested at all times. Do not expect significant protection in down markets from the latter, but expect pretty full participation during strong conditions.

Understanding a manager's investment style and philosophy is the key to forming better judgment of both past and future results. Some impertinent questions can help you achieve this understanding with specific **Manager Queries** (in italic type):

1. *Do your past periods of prosperity match with your investment style and with market leadership at those times?* For example, the manager who claims to be low risk but who was decimated in past down markets or who prospered mightily during highly speculative periods, such as early 1983, is certainly to be questioned. Compare that manager's record with his avowed style!

2. *Can you be expected to own the same kind of stocks as your assets under management grow substantially? Ask for the manager's list of stock holdings for a number of past years.* Look for the "less-deserved" (e.g., new-issue craze) profits described in Chapter 7; determine whether the securities or strategies that produced past success are practical to expect now!

3. *Do you make the industry bets you claim to?* You can check the veracity of a manager who denies being a "closet indexer"—essentially duplicating the S&P 500 in his stock holdings—*by asking for a chronolog-*

ical (quarterly) record of stock ownership sorted by industry over the past few years, as per Client Guide 6. Such a report will provide additional insights into the manager's risk-taking tendencies. For example, if he has held high percentages of portfolios in airlines, aluminums, steels, and the like, high volatility of returns is likely.

4. *Please provide your portfolio "turnover" figures*—statistics that indicate how much buying and selling of securities has occurred in the manager's accounts. Definitions of turnover vary. Just make sure you know what approximate percentage of your portfolio is apt to be altered in any given year. This knowledge will serve as another check against avowed manager style; it will also provide an idea of what to expect. If clients (particularly taxable ones) had asked for this information over the years, numerous lawsuits could have been avoided. Hyperactivity can be costly to any account, but to a taxable investor who has to pay heavy tax rates on short-term gains and high-enough penalties on long-term gains, the burden is onerous—and it should never come as a surprise.

In short, *demand specifics*. Ask whatever you need to corroborate manager claims and to give you a sense of comfort about how your money is likely to be handled.

Analyzing the People in an Investment Management Firm

A weak approach to the crucial analysis of management personnel would rely on platitudes, for example, emphasizing that intelligent, motivated, creative people operating in efficient environments are likely to be winners. While the description is valid, it hardly adds to your knowledge; after all, everybody knows that "you can't soar with the eagles if you're surrounded by turkeys!"

Since an investment firm is no better than its people, clients need to ignore the platitudes and, instead, be very specific in forming judgments of a manager group. Just as it is crucial to know your own investment personality, you must understand the approach and motivations of your investment manager. The manager questionnaire in Client Guide 2a can help you form this understanding, but deeper delving is also important if you are to find the best person to manage your investments. Interviews are a good means to this end, but remember, again, that such sessions will be most productive if *you, not the managers, control the interviews*.

Similarly, personal reference checking is important—and here, as in good reference work anywhere, the key is to go beyond the names provided you. Assume that references submitted represent persons certain to be positively inclined.

One way to check references is to *ask for names of former clients, especially those who have terminated their relationship with the firm recently*. While the investment advisory business is one that honors client confidentiality, corporate and other large funds' managers are generally a matter of public record. Although it is seldom done, you should ask for names of the organizations or individuals no longer clients and then initiate contact with the appropriate people to determine why the relationship was terminated. Caution is obviously in order here. You have chosen negatively inclined references, and clients are no better at admitting personal mistakes than managers. Highly informative to the reference checker is the date of termination, along of course with the former client's reason for manager dismissal. Did the termination occur mainly because better past results existed elsewhere? (Remember, they always do.) If the manager has the kind of composite performance file recommended, you can check to determine whether the former client jumped ship just prior to a strong performance recovery. It's important to bear in mind that even the best managers can occasionally have "jinxed" client relationships. A new account may enter a manager's stable at a time when the manager's purchases and sales are temporarily out of sync; the poor start can force manager "pressing," which, despite good intent, may simply compound the problem. Every manager has accounts at the top and bottom of his performance record, and it is possible that two clients with nearly identical objectives can have different experiences. Obviously, if too many clients are disenchanted or if there is a very wide band of performance results within a manager's control, there is great cause for caution.

Because of the vagaries of performance calculations, good reference checking should emphasize qualitative aspects of the manager. Some pertinent (they're not impertinent to the reference person you are contacting) questions include: Did they observe significant personnel turnover in the manager firm? Is one person within the group considerably weaker than others? (That person should be avoided as your direct portfolio manager.) What are the firm's strengths and weaknesses?

Your probing might also delve into the record of managers whose major investment management experience occurred in another organization. An individual might have one kind of short-term record with the firm you are considering, but you can enhance your knowledge about him by tracing his earlier record elsewhere. One two-person firm, which attracted a substantial client following in the early 1980s because of a fine 2-year record, offers a good illustration of how deeper investigating can reveal important insights. One of the two individuals had managed funds for another organization and had absolutely the worst performance experience of anyone in that firm for a number of years!

Aside from reference checking, one very useful way to assess a management firm is to break down its portfolio management and research teams, as shown in the Client Guide 9. Analyze the information and the handwritten inserts on this Guide.

Manager Query: Fill out the following form detailing the age and experience of your investment staff and the number of years each individual has worked with the firm.

If you are hoping for a longer-term relationship with a manager, you naturally should hope for a good age spread in his organization. You do not want all the important people hovering around their actuarial life expectancy, and you should be wary of an investment team made up of untested individuals—either inexperienced in the investment business itself or untried as a working group. Age spread can also tell you something about possible decision-making tendencies. A less experienced group might have trouble reacting to certain conditions, especially if the members have been exposed under fire to only one type of market

CLIENT GUIDE 9

An Investment Manager Personnel Profile Rating Form

Ownership Position within the Firm	Name of Individuals	Age	Years in Money Management Business	Years with This Firm	
	Portfolio Management Group				
Partner	William Chase	60	30	15	*Pretty "green"? 4 of the 6 managers have had limited experience together.*
Partner	John Sanborn	55	25	15	
	Frank Lea	50	20	2	
	Lydia Perrins	47	16	2	
	Lee Crosse	35	2	1	
	Robert Blackwell	30	1	1	
	Average	46	16	6	
	Research Group				
	Senior Analysts				
	Joseph Procter	62	40	15	*As with the portfolio group, mostly new faces in a new environment. Will they get along?*
	Edward Gamble	28	4	2	
	Evelyn Laurel	28	2	2	
	Frieda Hardy	26	1	1	
	Average	38	12	5	

Handwritten annotations:

- (near Age, Portfolio Management Group) *wonderful age spread*
- (near Years in Money Management) *some "young blood" along with experience*
- *But can people with 1-2 years experience truly manage money?*
- (near Senior Analysts) *Deceptive. One old-timer and 3 new-comers.*

condition. Barton Biggs of Morgan Stanley remarked in 1982 when he expected a long bull market with steadily expanding price/earnings multiples: "Make sure you have an 'old man' heavily involved in your portfolio's management." Having just been through a full decade of shrinking price/earnings multiples, Biggs felt that managers without the experience of the 1950s and 1960s—when price/earnings were rising— might tend to be shortsighted and sell good securities too soon. Biggs's advice went against conventional wisdom that older managers provide a more conservative investment strategy. Although the conclusion about rising multiples wasn't prescient until 1985, his approach was sound, because he remained open-minded and analyzed the logical implications of a portfolio team's background. He advocated the examination of age, personalities, philosophies, and experience, characteristics that also re-veal clues to the potential continuity or disruption of the organization itself.

Client Guide 9 also contains information on those who are owners of the firm. "The buck stops here" can mean a lot—it suggests incentives, willingness to stay, and so on.

Not included in the Guide is the consideration of past personnel turnover. A very important **Manager Query** should be: *What specific personnel changes have occurred in the important positions within your firm over the past 5 years?*

Of course, the investment manager can be a "lone wolf." He does not necessarily have to be part of a pack. It is logical, therefore, to determine whether you are seeking *an organization or an individual to manage your assets*. Investing is an "art" in which individuals can succeed without organizational structures behind them. As a matter of fact, the structures can be more of an impediment than an asset—many people are more productive without the group meetings that invariably exist internally in larger manager organizations. Likewise, managers subjected to minimal external interruptions of client meetings, marketing efforts, and consul-tant visits should have more time for what should be their central focus: investing your money wisely. Some of the world's best investors are either "lone wolves" or persons with limited staff support. The famed Warren Buffett of Omaha operates without a large, formalized research or portfolio management group, as have Henry Singleton of Teledyne and Larry Tisch of Loew's.

At some time, however, most successful managers have to rely on organizational functions. This is especially true in institutional investing because of the asset sizes involved and because of certain reporting responsibilities (questionnaires to be filled out, consultants and clients both being involved, etc.). Typical institutional investing doesn't lend itself to having a Tibetan recluse as a manager, however proficient he may be.

Hence, you need to delve beyond the surface of your intended manager. You need to understand his current and future *business strategy*, which is bound to affect how much time is spent on the (positive) investment process as opposed to (negative) marketing, client hand-holding, and other potential disruptions. Needless to say, the depth of investing firepower (the firm's personnel) should be proportional to assets under management and to the number and variety of clients served. Therefore, be sure to ask the following impertinent (*Manager Query*) questions:

1. *How many client relationships does each of your portfolio managers handle?* (Fifteen to twenty is considered a maximum comfortable number.)

2. *How many client meetings is each of your portfolio managers responsible for per year? Where are these meetings located?* If meetings are quarterly,* and if 25 percent of them are a plane ride away, a mere 15 clients could well absorb 10 to 20 percent of a manager's time.

3. *What other noninvestment duties are each portfolio manager's responsibility, and how much time is spent at these?*

4. *What sort of marketing effort are your portfolio managers engaged in?* Tracking a manager's client list is "fair game" and recommended as another clue to the manager's attention to investing as opposed to pursuits taking him away from portfolio management.

---

*Quarterly get-togethers are seldom that necessary or productive, but many clients cling to such schedules.

5. *What are the dissimilarities of your accounts?* It may not seem a bad indication that a manager handles all sorts of objectives, from high capital gain orientation all the way to high income requirements, but vast dissimilarities are potentially distracting—and they are difficult to accomplish.

CONCLUSIONS

While each manager should be given the opportunity to make his case in an organized fashion, *you* must control the process. The insights and specific questions in this chapter provide the preliminary substance necessary for the all-important examination of manager qualities.

11

CHOOSING THE
INVESTMENT
MANAGER
WINNERS:
EVALUATING
A MANAGER'S
STABILITY,
STRENGTHS, AND
WEAKNESSES

Though the topic is seldom broached by clients, an important clue to manager stability involves the delicate consideration of compensation. You cannot politely ask a manager exactly how much money he is making, but you are entitled to know enough to conclude whether he and his associates are likely to be around to manage your account in the future. Even in organizations where strategy is very similar among accounts, individuals make a difference. One person may be the strategy guru; others may be more proficient in stock selection; chemistry between a portfolio manager and the client can be a factor; and there are subtleties involved in day-to-day manager actions that can influence performance.

JUDGING A MANAGER ORGANIZATION'S STABILITY THROUGH ITS COMPENSATION LEVELS

If you really want the best to manage your money, it is incumbent on you to establish that the chief investment people will remain on board. For example, for years the banks and insurance companies have had to fight a major obstacle to manager longevity—*compensation*—finding it most difficult to compete with the unusually high monetary rewards common to the investment business. (Many portfolio managers, strategists, and research analysts are paid more than all but a few of a bank's or insurance company's top officers.) As a result, many financial institutions have set up subsidiary investment functions or joint ventures intended to make them competitive with pay scales and incentives available in other organizations; but many are still very vulnerable to loss of key personnel for a variety of financial reasons.

Loss of a crucial investment strategist can be very costly to you. First, the disruption can obviously affect decision making—and performance. Secondly, the change can be doubly expensive if the departing person is replaced by someone with different philosophies, leading to costly portfolio shifting (through both trading and commission costs). *Many portfolios have suffered expensive restructurings as a result of personnel changes, without the client's knowledge or consent*. A number of New York banks have gone through just such shifting. One went through a painful and expensive switch out of growth stocks when a new chief investment officer was hired only to reverse the strategy when this individual left the bank 18 months later. A San Francisco institution did something similar, shifting from a value-oriented portfolio approach to a fast-trading, market-timing ploy and then back to value-growth style—all within 5 years and all because they had three different leaders over this span.

Client Guide 10 provides a reasonable approach for a client to take with the compensation issue.

Manager Query: Our understanding is that pay structures within your industry are as follows. Please indicate to us how you and the people with greatest impact on your investment decision making and on our account are compensated as compared with these figures. (You might also ask the manager to confirm that the figures presented as the norm are the norm.)

CLIENT GUIDE 10
Investment Manager "Scorecard" on
Compensation Levels of Key Personnel

Title	Our Understanding of "Normal" Compensation for This Position Is	Your Personal and Organization Compensation for These Roles			
		Below	Average	Above	Way Above
You personally	$250,000				
Your back-up on our account	150,000				
Key investment strategist	350,000		(Please check)		
Portfolio managers	350,000				
Research analysts	125,000				

The trend of sales to or mergers of investment management firms with banks, insurance companies, and other organizations places a new burden on clients, who deserve to assess whether the new ownership provides the incentives for the most important individuals to produce as they did before. Will the sudden riches from the sale/merger cause a change in work style? Employment agreements are normally involved, but attorneys will tell you that enforceability is limited; besides, you cannot force conscientiousness, devotion, desire, and other crucial qualities. Will the firm and its key people have the autonomy they had before? Will the buyer demand new "products" or responsibilities which will interfere with their normal duties?

What this then demands is a client approach similar to Client Guide 10 on compensation. You may not be privy to all financial aspects of the ownership change, but you certainly are entitled to know enough about the deal to conclude whether the important manager personnel have adequate incentives to stay on and work as diligently as they did before. The best "handcuffs" are large hard-dollar incentives to remain on board—something a client should understand. The sale that pays mainly up front (to the manager organization) or that leaves relatively little on the back side for the key people is a suspicious one. This sort of information should be demanded by clients of managers going this route.

Of course, financial reward is not the only factor affecting longevity and continuity within an organization. Ownership, work environment, perquisites, challenges, prestige, and even office location are additional factors once an adequate monetary level has been attained. So, dig deep enough to know whether the total motivations are adequate. Use the Client Guide to get a current compensation picture, but use it also to track the manager's stability and internal mobility over time. The Guide, combined with Client Guide 9 (showing manager personnel by chronological age, investment experience, longevity with the firm, and ownership position), can also serve as a model from which you can query how personnel are apt to move internally in the future. By doing so, you will gain special insights into the possibility of the leopard's changing its spots—at your expense—in the future.

JUDGING MANAGER STRENGTHS AND WEAKNESSES

Investment management firms will bombard clients with reasons for hiring them. The clients' responsibility is to treat the claims with circumspection—to engage in the most effective impertinent questioning, which means speaking softly but carrying a big stick.

An excellent starting point is to determine *whether a manager knows his investor self*.

Clients should delve into the attitudes, goals, and sense of realism of managers. Do they "have it all together" in their work? Are they aware of their strengths and weaknesses? Do they understand that they may have to change their approach with the times (e.g., to cope with the problems of larger sums under their management or with economic conditions they have never experienced before)?

An important part of managers' knowing themselves involves scrupulously avoiding investment areas where they are not particularly knowledgeable, where they are not sufficiently comfortable, or where they possess no real "leg up" on the competition. For instance, how many firms that have concentrated on domestic stocks would do well at international investing? A distinct minority! This fact, however, didn't halt an investment firm in the early 1970s from placing 20 to 30 percent of its portfolios in stocks from practically every foreign market of the world. Companies they could hardly have known, operating in conditions they were ill equipped to analyze, suddenly became the foundation for their portfolios. Their thesis was not one of bearishness about the United States or about world conditions or currency movements. They had been good stock "pickers" over the years, but their success had come from being exceptional interviewers and analyzers of corporate managers. This was hardly a transferable talent, since their domestic experience was little help to them when dealing with international language barriers, accounting practices, and security markets. They *were* professionals—but in *their* home base, something both they and their clients recognized only after significant losses were incurred.

It is dangerous to alter investment style radically; the probabilities are against becoming proficient in a very different style without suffering an expensive learning period (if you ever learn the new approach at all).

Therefore, you should labor to ascertain a firm's realistic strengths and weaknesses. You will no doubt have heard about the strengths, so you should plan to concentrate on the manager's shortfalls. One thing is certain: A manager who does not understand his frailties is certainly not going to overcome them. Some of the clues to such weaknesses have already been discussed; for example, a manager's not knowing how and why he is doing well or poorly, or not understanding that he may have certain destructive investing habits, such as handling either gains or losses particularly badly. A manager may emphasize short-term gains so much that he never achieves the big wins that may take years to develop, or he may consistently deal with losses by selling out at the bottom.

Determine, also, whether managers are willing to "keep up." The organization that shrugs off serious theories, with apparently no willingness to support any negative conclusions, becomes the "ole gray mare" that will probably soon not be what it used to be. A recent example of this was the controversy surrounding MPT, discussed in Chapters 6 and 9. A manager's gut feeling might have been that the theory was too weak, too controversial, or too complicated, but it behooved him to understand the principles before damning them. Rigidity when confronted with new ideas is to be avoided—and, of course, knowing what ideas others are embracing is an important strategic investment ploy.

An extension of strength and weakness analysis includes a "personality search." Have the people within the manager organization explored the differences in their philosophies (which invariably exist)? Being sensitive to the natural inclinations and idiosyncrasies of your counterparts is one way to mold a good team.

LOOK FOR A SENSE OF DISCIPLINE IN THE MANAGER ORGANIZATION

Infinite wisdom is hard to find in the investment business. Even if one individual possesses exceptional investing insights, it is hard to transfer those talents and have them translated well through others. (Even well translated, they may not be accepted.) The variables of the investment management business demand discipline. Think of the thousands of securities from which a portfolio manager can choose and consider the security price fluctuations that occur daily. Add to this the many factors bearing on both the fundamentals and the market prices. It is truly overwhelming.

The narrow specialist can handle these variables by owning only a small number of securities in a limited number of industries. Most management firms, however particularly those with large sums to manage— require greater diversity in investments. Their task then is to make sure that the multitude of demands and distractions (which include marketing, client contact, management of their business, etc.) do not consume them. Following are some disciplines that have helped the better management firms stay on top:

1.   Separating the universe of industries available for investment according to their supply/demand positions. Practically every business finds its critical supply/demand balance skewed from time to time. Not enough investors think in these practical terms; even those who do normally need some "props" to remind them of the inevitable cycles.

2.   Understanding the expectations of others. The stock market is one huge "voting booth," and anything an investor can do to know what others are anticipating provides a clue to potential prices. While polling investment opinions is subjective, investing without understanding the extent and direction of the general market's popularity or that of a particular stock is like firing a gun without sufficient ammunition.

3.   Supervising accounts in an efficient manner. Poring over computer runs is tedious and tiring. Even 8 or 10 accounts can be arduous to supervise if not presented well, so you can imagine how a few dozen portfolios, each with numerous holdings, can become a blur. All the necessary filters should be available, and they should be clearly presented and well organized so that the tedium is minimized, and so that managers can concentrate adequately on their individual stock holdings, investment strategy, and account structure.

4.   Valuations of individual securities—intended to separate the most attractive from the least attractive—should be equally sensible. No human mind can track all the market changes that affect relative values. A logical system, presented simply, is another discipline that exists in almost every fine investment organization.

5.   Good "exception reporting" should exist. Managers should know when portfolios become unevenly structured as compared to in-house models and accounts with similar objectives. Managers should also program themselves to know when their cohorts might be changing opinions. This last point may seem strange, but organizations holding positions in scores of securities cannot discuss each one every day—and changing prices and new information are constantly influencing judgments. Hence an internal discipline that forces managers to restate their conviction (to hold, buy more, or sell existing positions) is essential for consistency and just plain good portfolio management.

Focus on whether "hard" decisions are encouraged throughout the organization. Lack of conviction is likely to create mediocre results. (You might as well be indexed.) Are research analysts merely staff people, having little direct impact on final decisions? Is the firm overly dependent on outside (brokerage) research?

Analyzing a manager's decision-making process, therefore, includes understanding discipline. Too many manager organizations are undisciplined to the point where Mike finds out from Fred that he is buying X and selling Y when they happen to meet in the men's room!

There are many more disciplines characteristic of efficient organizations. Probing the examples given, plus others, can be a fine way to judge the winners of the future.

Time is bound to be an obstacle to your manager probing. You have only so many hours to devote to it, and managers have only so many to offer. Your goal should be to find the manager with whom you are most comfortable, hoping at the same time to find the individual or organization with unique and admirable qualities. Keep asking yourself: What makes this manager unique? Is it the brilliance of one or two individuals, or is it the internal disciplines that cause a group to behave very intelligently? Does this firm or individual have a superior way of forming investment strategies, conducting research, and making decisions?

The preceding points should produce the most important insights you'll need to make a well-informed decision. For those who would like to dig deeper into investment manager analysis, I've also included the following elements to consider and some additional Manager Queries to pose:

Manager Query: What weaknesses do you have that might be corrected? And what are you doing about them?

To illustrate, our portfolio management group recognized a failing of not being as good at buying out-of-favor stocks as we thought we might be. So we set out to correct this weakness, and we can explain our solutions to clients. It might or might not satisfy them, but either way the dialogue should prove useful to them in assessing us.

Determine whether the manager acknowledges the same weaknesses that your independent reference checking revealed. If they are the same, ask: How do you plan to correct your failings? And conclude yourself whether his remedies seem to be effective. If the manager's perceptions of weaknesses are different from your research, determine why.

Manager Query: Does your firm conduct any true "research and development?"

Effective research and development (R&D) is important to growing companies and to those engaged in complicated areas, such as investment management. Contrary to common belief, few money managers engage in much, if any, developmental research at all. Managers may make large expenditures in financial (security) analysis, but this is more akin to another industry's product development and purchasing departments. Most work follows traditional security analysis, and little is done uniquely. Precious little effort is allocated to work that produces new methods or anything close to so-called basic research.

Some of the best firms show more foresight, however. They are willing to spend money researching out-of-the-ordinary ideas, particularly ways of enhancing their collection of data and unique information. Not enough management firms have developed new procedures as has, for example, Dean LeBaron's Batterymarch. Batterymarch utilizes *no* traditional security analysis. It harnesses the computer for its stock selection and for its day-to-day buying and selling of securities.

Recognizing what good R&D is can make the difference between superior performance in the future and mediocrity, or worse. So ask the blunt questions here to separate those who are likely to set the standards for the future from those who are liable to remain pedestrian.

Manager Query: Have you organized yourself so that running your business is not interfering with the function of investing?

Has your organization provided for professional management of back office/clerical, personnel, library, accounting, data processing? Beware of firms with individuals wearing too many "hats": The Peter Principle, which states that efficiency breaks down as specialized people assume responsibilities that are not within their expertise, certainly applies to the investment function.

Manager Query: Is your organization promising to be all things to all people?

Do not expect an admission of this. You have to determine for yourself whether the manager handles high-income-requirement accounts along with growth portfolios; as indicated, since stock selection and portfolio structures are bound to be very different in these two objectives, few managers succeed at both. Similarly, discover whether the manager is advising many different account types with sharply varying objectives— that is, individual, taxable accounts of all sizes and objectives, along with many tax-free, institutional clients.

Manager Query: Are you aware of, and sensitive to, the competition from other investments?

For example, if bonds are yielding 13 to 14 percent—well above what common stocks have returned historically and well above interest rates that have prevailed in the United States over the years—shouldn't equity managers be aware of the competition from this source? If real estate seems destined to return either more or less than what might be reasonably expected from stocks, won't this have an effect on flow of investor funds to and from these two assets? Certainly managers should have insights into the relative prospects of competitive investments.

Manager Query: Are you a "bottom-up" stock selection enthusiast, concentrating mainly on company developments without contemplating many other considerations, or do broader economic factors influence your individual stock selection?

It is useful to assess how adept your manager is in forecasting the general economy, broad industry trends, or whatever drives his decision making.

Manager Query: How do you wade through overly complicated inputs in making your investment decisions?

Clients should determine how managers eliminate "noise" from too many inputs—yet get enough of the important variables to make diverse decisions in a changing world.

The following are suggestions to help you judge this kind of manager effectiveness:

1. Understand how the organization communicates internally. *Are there efficient ways to ensure that the decision makers are equally well-informed?*
2. Discover how they make decisions and *how they follow up on them*.
3. Analyze their use of the computer or other aids to improve and simplify stock selection *and* portfolio management. Ask to see all the internal aids and come to your own conclusion.

Manager Query: *Are you well-rounded as an investment person?*

Does the manager have a "scope" that might be useful to you in some way or that might give you clues to his potential longevity as a fine investor? You may not hire a manager for tasks beyond making money in one specific asset type. But you might envision accruing special insights through your association that will lead to extra values for you. The manager might, for example, be able to advise you on interest rates and help you with your financing plans, provide excellent advice on asset mix decisions, or introduce you to an asset vehicle that might prove valuable to your overall results. If you are looking for these extras, be sure that your manager is a thinking person, one who will understand your business and be sensitive to your special needs. This is not to imply that you should hire a portfolio manager mainly to help you solve *other* problems, nor do you want a manager who is a jack of all trades but not a master of his own. The manager's talents in money management, however, may be supplemented by some broader useful knowledge that in turn provides you with important clues to his *thinking process*. Articles written, or "professional contributions," can provide other clues. Since thinking is the major asset you are buying in a manager, scope can be a sound selection criterion.

CONCLUSIONS

You now have both the general advice and specific aids to separate the swift from the slow, the strong from the weak investment managers. You should be able to engage in manager selection with a knowledge and preparedness that are bound to help you make far better decisions. The easy way out is to be obsessed with and rely solely on past performance data. The best way is to base your choice on solid performance analysis along with an intelligent use of qualitative judgments. This will require additional time, but it will be time well spent if you follow the impertinent questioning examples given. Only this way will you truly know, in Damon Runyon's words, "how to bet."

12
MANAGER FEES— REASONABLE OR EXCESSIVE?

Always those that dance must pay the music

John Taylor
Taylor's Feast

One of the reasons the investment management business has been so profitable *for managers* is the naiveté about fees on the part of so many clients. While practically everyone who has ever employed an investment manager has inquired about costs before signing a contract, very few clients sufficiently understand the very important obstacles and implications of manager fees.

Fees, of course, cannot be efficiently judged *before* the money is invested. One cannot expect exactness from a service that is *inexact*. Investing is not like buying gasoline, for example, where the differences between self-service, mini-service, and full service are abundantly clear (although the author finds he gets equal absence of service from all three!). More personal than gasoline, services such as accounting and income tax preparation show a more predictable relationship between value received and charges made.

Investment management fee considerations need *not* remain as muddled as they are today. A more skeptical and knowledgeable market—with better-informed clients—is one important solution.

One obstacle to client sophistication is the almost universally accepted axiom that fees are among the least important investment management considerations. Indeed, managers, consultants, and clients alike generally agree that fees pale in importance compared to the wide differences in ultimate investment results. Most contend, "Why bother ourselves with differences of small fractions of a percent in annual fees when divergence in performance results might be 4 or 5 percent or even higher? Isn't concentration on fees being penny wise and pound foolish?"

Chapter 6's discussion of stock market efficiency and the construction of indexed investment portfolios considered whether you should rely on managers' having large incremental performance above the general market. As indicated, although apparently less than half of the managers have exceeded returns from the S&P, many *have* provided superior results over long periods of time with benefits amounting to significant multiples of the fees charged. Thus, while *fees are important*, they certainly *should not be the paramount consideration. The probability of strong performance should be your major concern. Since, however, fees are normally fixed and future performance results are con, ctural, you should not close your eyes to costs, either.*

The startling effects of compounding returns on money illustrate the need for more attention to such management costs. Assume that two $1 million portfolios exist and that both grow, *before fees*, at slightly over 10 percent per year for 20 years. Assume that one portfolio has a manager who charges 0.5 percent annually and that the other has one who receives 1.5 percent. The lower-fee portfolio's value *after fees* amounts to slightly over $6 million in the twentieth year, while the higher-fee list totals about $1 million less, at slightly over $5 million. If a manager's fee schedule cries out, "I'm expensive," perhaps you ought to believe it! *The fact is that the smokescreen surrounding management fees is so thick that most clients do not insist on deducting fees from reported performance results.* Hence, most clients are not making accurate assessments of either their absolute returns or their performance relative to others. Although neither managers nor investors are fond of gambling analogies, the more the "house" takes, the lower are the probabilities for "player" success, especially over longer periods of time.

Aside from the direct costs, there are some deeper inferences that should be drawn from fees. For the very level of managers' fees implies attitudes and expectations on the part of both clients and managers— attitudes and expectations that often determine the success or failure of the manager/client relationship, which in turn often determines the final investment result!

Manager fee schedules make a statement. They tell a story about the manager organization, including possibly its own investing style, its risk-taking posture, and even its future. To illustrate, a very low fee (e.g., 0.25 percent annually) may be like the "free" cheese in a mousetrap. Low fees raise the following questions:

1. Will the low-fee firm have to service more accounts or manage more money than one charging higher fees? Will you get the attention and supervision you deserve?

2. Will the low-fee manager be as profitable as the similarly situated firm with a more aggressive fee schedule? Will this mean that the former cannot attract or keep outstanding individuals?

3. Does the very low fee suggest a mediocrity (or even inferiority) complex that is likely to affect performance results?

4.   Will a low-fee firm have the money to spend on computers, research, and other aids that might contribute to investment success?

In contrast, here are questions raised by an exceedingly high fee (anything over 1 percent):

1.   Is the firm highly opportunistic? Is it attracting clients with such high expectations that the business lacks stability over time? Remember, high turnover of accounts leads to manager nervousness, more time spent on marketing, and other disruptions that are detrimental to good portfolio management.

2.   Will the firm's owners become so prosperous that they pay less attention to the business? (Not everyone handles nouveaux riches in a way that benefits those who have contributed to the affluence—there are countless cases where *manager* living style changes have *far exceeded client attainments.**) It is possible that the bulk of a higher fee goes for "productive" uses. But this isn't as probable as you'd like to think. Take the unfortunate case where a marketing representative of a manager firm received about half of very high fees paid by new accounts. Clients were paying substantially more for the firm's marketing than they were for the management support system, which was hardly developed at all. This firm's profitability soared, but its clients fared badly with very poor investment results.

It is true that you often get what you pay for in investment management, as evidenced by the relatively poor records of many low-fee institutions and by the spectacular records of certain hedge funds despite their exceptionally high fees. Generally speaking, however, there are higher risks to clients who pay very high fees. *All things being equal,*

---

*The thought of investment people benefiting more than their clients was more aptly stated in a famous book, published in 1940, titled *Where Are the Customers' Yachts?* by Fred Scheed, Jr. (republished in 1960 in *Space Age Additions*).

the higher the expenses, the more a management firm must demonstrate its "superiority." As Peter Vermilye, former chief investment officer of Citibank, stated: "If you cost more, you have to show you can walk on water." Of course, no two management organizations are exactly equal, which is why the consideration of fees belongs in your qualitative manager assessment process. Furthermore, there is a big difference between a spread of 1 percent annual fees and 0.125 or even 0.25 percent. *Allowing very small fractions to tilt one's head is being shortsighted.*

There are factors that have a bearing on "deserved" fees. These include the following:

Manager Queries:

1.   *Which individual is managing your account? (An unproven manager even within a proven organization can be suspect.)*
2.   *How many accounts do the firm and your individual manager handle? (The more is not the merrier.)*
3.   *Does the fee include services beyond portfolio management? (If the organization acts as custodians of securities or, in the case of individual investors, if it provides tax advice or unusually fine tax shelter leadership, higher fees are deserved.)*

Fees normally vary according to the size of your managed assets; charges are normally "front-end loaded," with higher percentages meted against smaller portfolios and with decreasing fee percentages charged for larger amounts. A 0.75 or 1 percent annual fee is very normal for accounts under $2 million, but this would be a high fee for $10 million and a *very* high fee for a portfolio of over $10 million.

The following is a framework for your use in assessing manager fees. It will help you understand fee "vibrations"—what attitudes and expectations are suggested by specific fee levels. The first example generalizes about manager and client attitudes and expectations for a $10 million equity or balanced account (excluding a pure fixed-income account). This is followed by two matrices (Client Guides 11 and 11a) that analyze fee levels for fixed-income and equity portfolios of many account sizes.

Fee (As Annual Percentage of Assets Managed)	"Vibrations"—How High the Fee Appears and What It Might Suggest about Manager and Client
0.125	Manager *must* be insecure. All the negative questions posed earlier about very low fees are pertinent. Client probably looking for a bargain and is likely instead to get what he is paying for.
0.25	Certainly the low end of fees for most managers. Again, check out the low-fee warnings.
0.375	Still low. But the lower-fee warnings can now be muted.
0.5	This is close to the industry standard (for $10 million accounts).
0.75	At this fee level (and above), expectations of both client and manager are above average.
1	This fee demands that clients check their objectives. Are fairly dramatic (perhaps unrealistic) returns being anticipated? Are you buying higher risk than you can afford or tolerate?
1.5 or higher	Probabilities are that you have been attracted to what appears to be a great *recent* record. Caveat emptor!

Time now for Client Guides 11 and 11a, two matrices that highlight the most likely signals emanating from various fee levels for varying amounts of bond and stock money managed—for accounts ranging from $250,000 up. Fees for portfolios below $250,000 are not included because: (1) it is often difficult for investors to find competent, interested advisers for smaller amounts; (2) the charges for individual attention are often so high that clients are better off investing through no-load mutual funds; or (3) the fees are very hard to quantify because they are "hidden" in syndications or other vehicles with complicated (and generally excessive) charges.

CLIENT GUIDE 11
Manager Fees—What Do They Suggest?
for
Equity or Balanced Accounts[a]

Annual Fee on Cumulative Total Dollars Managed, as a percentage of 1%

Dollars under Management (in millions)									"Signals" from the Various Fee Levels	
0.25	0.50	1	5	10	20	30	50	100	Manager	Client
0.50	0.30	0.30	0.25	0.20	0.15	0.125	0.125	0.125	Insecure	Low expectations
0.50	0.375	0.375	0.35	0.30	0.25	0.20	0.20	0.15	Must be taking many accounts	Check low-fee warnings
0.75	0.40	0.40	0.375	0.35	0.30	0.25	0.225	0.20	Still not promising much	Moderate goals

169

CLIENT GUIDE 11
Manager Fees—What Do They Suggest?
for
Equity or Balanced Accounts[a]

Annual Fee on Cumulative Total Dollars Managed, as a percentage of 1%

Dollars under Management (in millions)									"Signals" from the Various Fee Levels	
0.25	0.50	1	5	10	20	30	50	100	Manager	Client
1.0	1.0	0.75	0.60	0.50	0.45	0.40	0.375	0.30	Realistic (average) self-image	Medium expectations
1.40	1.25	1.00	0.75	0.70	0.60	0.50	0.45	0.40	Slightly above average	Slightly above average expectations
1.50	1.50	1.25	1.00	0.80	0.70	0.60	0.55	0.45	Promising very good results	Looking for fine results
2.00	1.50	1.50	1.25	1.25	1.10	1.00	0.85	0.75	Promising dramatic gains	Manager has to invest very wisely
Over 2.00	2.00	2.00	1.50	1.35	1.25	1.00	0.90	0.85	Super confident (un-realistic?)	Reaching for the "rainbow"

[a]Balanced accounts in which the manager is expected to make the shifts between bonds and stocks (not simply directed in the balance ratio by the client) generally demand an equity-type fee. Clients normally avoid creating manager conflicts of interest that can exist when one asset (of the manager's choice) produces a different compensation level than another asset.

CLIENT GUIDE 11a
Manager Fees—What Do They Suggest?
for
Fixed Income Accounts

Annual Fee on Cumulative Total Dollars Managed, as a percentage of 1%

Dollars under Management (in millions)									"Signals" from the Various Fee Levels	
0.25	0.50	1	5	10	20	30	50	100	Manager	Client
0.30	0.25	0.125	0.125	0.125	0.10	0.10	0.10	0.10	Insecure	Low expectations
0.35	0.30	0.20	0.15	0.15	0.125	0.125	0.125	0.125	Must be taking many accounts	Check low-fee warnings
0.40	0.35	0.25	0.20	0.175	0.15	0.15	0.15	0.15	Still not promising much	Moderate goals

CLIENT GUIDE 11a
Manager Fees—What Do They Suggest?
for
Fixed Income Accounts

Annual Fee on Cumulative Total Dollars Managed, as a percentage of 1%

Dollars under Management (in millions)									"Signals" from the Various Fee Levels	
0.25	0.50	1	5	10	20	30	50	100	Manager	Client
0.75	0.75	0.63	0.50	0.35	0.25	0.20	0.20	0.20	Realistic (average) self-image	Medium expectations
1.0	1.0	0.75	0.60	0.50	0.40	0.30	0.25	0.25	Slightly above average	Slightly above average expectations
1.0	1.0	0.80	0.70	0.45	0.40	0.40	0.35	0.35	Promising very good results	Looking for fine results
1.20	1.20	1.00	0.80	0.60	0.50	0.50	0.45	0.45	Promising dramatic gains	Manager has to invest very wisely
Over 1.25	1.25	1.25	1.00	0.75	0.63	0.55	0.50	0.50	Superconfident (unrealistic?)	Reaching for the "rainbow"

To repeat, fees may be secondary to other investment management considerations, but they may not be quite as secondary as assumed by many clients. In fact, fee schedules provide important clues to your chances for success in the future. Besides, the probabilities are high that you *can* find a very good manager at a reasonable (not the cheapest or most exorbitant) fee structure. As A.G. Olsen, director of employee financial programs at Abbott Laboratories, says: "Manager choice is not unlike that of your doctor. You certainly don't make a selection by seeking the lowest fee. Yet, unless you have a very rare illness or surgical need, you can probably find competent aid without paying the highest, exorbitant fees, either."

GETTING THE MOST FROM YOUR INVESTMENT MANAGER; PLUS, HOW TO BE A MORE ASTUTE CLIENT

13

JUDGING MANAGERS' QUALITIES AFTER YOU HAVE HIRED THEM:

Assessing Managers' Actions

To know you is to love you—or is it?
One of life's
most challenging queries

177

Just as performance numbers and fees should not be the sole criteria for manager selection, reported figures alone should not determine whether you retain a manager's services. Indeed, it can make sense for you to fire a manager who has produced decent results, just as it may be wise to hire or retain a manager with a mediocre or (occasionally) even a poor record. In all cases, incisive questioning, leading to good qualitative judgments, is crucial.

Chapters 10 and 11 explained how you should probe beyond the figures to pick a manager. Obviously, a great deal of this same advice is pertinent to the decision whether to maintain or cut an existing adviser. If you have a manager in place, however, you have considerably more information at your disposal to help you decide whether to continue the relationship.

Here, then, are three additional suggestions intended for anyone having close access to managers.

Understanding Your Manager's Proficiency by Analyzing His Actions

Investment managers' actions always speak louder than their words. While performance figures constitute the most measurable of manager actions, other factors may provide the best clues to *future* results.

A good example of analyzing manager actions is to know how and why money has been made or lost in your account. Some of this was covered in the discussion of performance statistics, but there are additional worthwhile approaches. One is to follow your manager's purchases and sales, looking for patterns. Regardless of manager investing style, there is much to be learned from intelligent scrutiny of a manager's trading. The task has its complications, but either the manager should supply the information to help you make this assessment or you should construct a system for yourself.

A "trading analysis" of your account—a compilation that concludes success or failure from a long-term record of purchases and sales made in your account and that simultaneously contrasts these moves with the market's behavior over the same period—can provide valuable insights. We use just such a program in our firm, one that assumes that each purchase or sale is accompanied by a like theoretical investment or sale in the S&P 500 Stock Index. A running tabulation then reveals how well our buys and sells have done relative to the market. Weighted for dollar amounts, the program reveals how much our activity added to or detracted from the portfolio's total performance over the period covered. If the purchases are up 15 percent while the S&P rose just 5 percent, the difference of 10 percent obviously indicates good selection. If the sales, however, subsequently advance 22 percent while the S&P rises only 2 percent, the selling clearly weakened results by 20 percent. In this case, since the manager's overall activity detracted from results by 10 percent, he would have been better off doing nothing.

Another way to attain a sense of your manager's capabilities is to plot his major purchases on a stock chart, such as that shown in Figure 13.1 (Client Guide 12). Each time your manager purchases or sells a security, you mark the percentage of your portfolio traded at that time on a price chart as illustrated. For example, assume that in March 1981 you receive notification that your adviser has committed 1.5 percent of your account to a purchase of Digital Equipment (DEC) stock. You simply note a "B 1 5" (for "buy 1.5 percent") at the March 1981, approximate $90 market price point (scale left) on the bottom line (the line connected by open squares) of the three graph lines of the guide. Extend this mark up to the second and third lines. The top line (connected by crosses) plots DEC stock's action relative to the general market (the S&P 500, scale right); the middle line (connected by "diamonds") plots DEC's earnings per share, also relative to the S&P. Your "record" has begun.

The next time a trade takes place in DEC, do the same. In our Client Guide example, the next activity in the stock occurred on June 30, 1982, when 0.7 percent of your portfolio (approximately half your DEC holding) was sold at about $75—see "S 0.7" on the Guide. Although the stock had dropped sharply since its purchase, you should know whether it was the overall market or your manager's selection which caused the result. By extending the sale point up to the top line and then comparing that line's purchase and sale points, you can see that DEC stock had done worse than the S&P (which must have fallen sharply between March 1981 and June 30, 1982) by about 10%. So the plotting has already given you more perspective than you would have had without it!

180

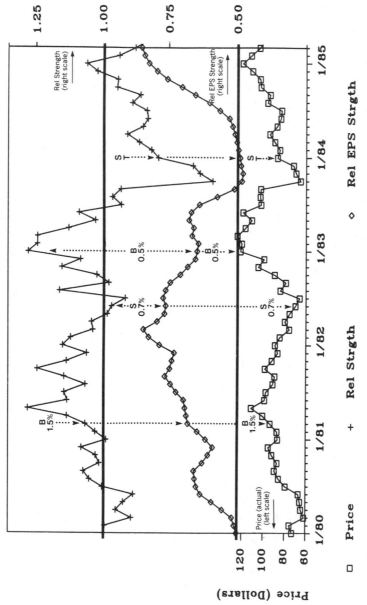

Figure 13.1. Client Guide 12: DEC Relative Strength versus S&P 500 (data as of August 31, 1985).

Then, in January 1983, your manager "B 0.5" (buys 0.5 percent) at $100, after DEC had experienced both a large absolute and a large relative (to the S&P) price gain. Finally, on January 1, 1984, the "S T" ("sold total") means that your total holding was liquidated at $70, after another poor absolute and relative performance.

The Guide delineates just how poorly your adviser did with your ownership of DEC. Your manager bought high and sold low twice, and you obviously lost money because of this. The markings on relative market strength confirm how badly he did; although his first trade wasn't as bad on a relative basis as it looked on an absolute basis, your manager's first move wasn't good and subsequent trades were worse. This was not the case of a stock's declining only through an overall poor general market environment.

The markings on the middle line provide additional perspective. They show how DEC's earnings were progressing or retrogressing at the manager's different points of buying and selling. Comparing the manager's two purchase points, DEC's earnings experience was decidedly negative to that of the S&P.

One stock does not a portfolio make, however! To isolate your manager's poor timing and/or misfortune with Digital is secondary to assessing your total portfolio's results. Tracking activity this way does, however, provide valuable clues to your manager's capabilities. Just as you judge a friend by actions over time and sense important traits, such as honesty and loyalty, tracking your manager's actions in the most significant dealings (highest percentage holdings) can help you assess money-making capabilities. It is a great offset to short memories and a fine way to determine whether excuses for poor performance are justified.

Another valuable ploy is to determine whether the manager has been right (or wrong) in the past, *and for what reasons*. Although luck plays its part in investing, you should strive to rely on chance as little as possible. It is important, therefore, to gauge whether there is a consistency between investment results and the reasons for successes or failures.

One way to assess your manager's depth and perceptiveness is to track his judgments. Here you should differentiate between a manager's proficiency in forecasting such broad fundamentals as the economy, inflation, and interest rates, and his ability to evaluate the fundamentals that determine the inherent value of your holdings (buildup of profits, book value, cash flow and dividends of stocks owned). The former, very broad forecasts can be indicative of intellectual excellence, but they generally will not "pay the rent" as well as an accurate assessment of your securities' values. The temptation, however, is often to concentrate on neither of these fundamentals but, instead, to focus on a stock's immediate returns as a way of judging success or failure. In fact, longer view and good assessment of (particularly a stock's) fundamentals are often ultimately more rewarding. Even if current performance numbers look discouraging, if a stock's fundamentals are improving, there's a good chance the market will catch up and reward your patience and that of your manager.

One very astute investment client, R. H. (Tad) Jeffrey, wrote a provocative article* in which he insisted that a client should be less concerned with immediate returns and more interested in his portfolio's progress in earnings and dividends over a longer period of time. Jeffrey admits that there are limits to this philosophy: For example, managers who pay way too much for purchases (of earnings and dividends) are committing their clients to very long waits for the fundamentals to develop and earn recognition from the market. Paying too much obviously also exposes an account to near-term (and possibly long-term) market depreciation.

Jeffrey's thesis may advise a longer view than most investors would be comfortable with, but there is merit in it; clients should not close their eyes to the course of fundamentals in the securities they own. (The middle line of Client Guide 12 was inserted for this very reason—to track fundamentals along with market prices.)

In Chapter 7, an example was given of a manager who received sudden performance credit for a long-awaited emergence of cyclical stocks (where fundamental improvements had not occurred and were not even yet occurring). The conclusion was obvious: Despite a (short) period of good performance, the manager's judgment was not to be applauded. Another example would be many of the "gold bug" heroes of the

---

*"Internal Portfolio Growth: The Better Measure," *Journal of Portfolio Management,* summer edition, 1977.

mid-1970s. History shows that most gold advocates had been forecasting rising gold prices for many years. They had been wrong on a relative basis (relative to other investments) and had actually been wrong on an absolute basis, too. (Annualized returns from holding gold from the early 1930s to 1973 approximated only 4 percent per year.) Then, as a result of two events, the Middle East conflict and the oil embargo—events on which few gold bugs had predicated their forecasts—gold prices surged. Most gold bugs, then, were right for the wrong reasons. But this unassailable truth did not stop investors around the world from hailing almost every "bug" as a guru. I also remember the case of a manager who bet heavily on three Japanese stocks based on his forecast of the three companies showing excellent operating improvement. He was dead wrong on their profits, but a sudden change in the relationship between the yen and the U.S. dollar—which he had not anticipated—made him appear to be a skilled investor.

You would obviously be misguided to favor a manager whose success stemmed from *unsuccessful* forecasting, even if it produced unanticipated good fortune. Similarly, you should think twice before firing a manager who had correctly anticipated fundamentals (e.g., correctly predicting earnings of important stock holdings) and yet who suffered because the improvements have not been appreciated.

Wrong decisions, therefore, deserve analysis, too. Were those who sold growth stocks early in 1971, prior to the rising of those prices to ridiculous heights, really wrong? Many were damned or considered inept for a year or so, until the market regained its sanity, at which time they again appeared prescient. The fine management firm of Capital Guardian lost hundred of millions of dollars of accounts in the early 1970s mainly because they didn't participated in the Nifty Fifty madness. Are those who sold technology stocks in certain of their heydays, at prices that bore no semblance to fundamentals, to be criticized for experiencing short periods of underperformance?

Consistent investment success, with minimal risk, normally follows the recognition of sound and reasonably accurate forecasts of trends. The ultimate comes when strong fundamentals are finally recognized by investors. But, as emphasized in Chapter 5 on cycles and styles, this very investor recognition is bound to be imprecise—one strong reason why you should dig deeper. Market acceptance of an industry group or individual stocks is often slow in coming, but just as often its eventual arrival is like an eruption. Since you certainly don't want to lose faith in a manager immediately before "recognition time," your analysis of his reasoning and forecasts of fundamentals can be invaluable.

Learning from Your Manager's Handling of Gains and Losses

A final qualitative assessment involves a manager's behavior pattern in handling gains and losses. As Peter L. Bernstein said: "It is crucial to see whether the (inevitable) mistakes and successes are handled in a manner consistent with the manager's avowed style and strategy."

Starting with loss considerations, it is important to understand how adversity is managed. Does your manager cut his losses short (keep them small by liquidating before they become very large)? Or does he have the conviction to add to less successful holdings at lower prices? This is not meant to imply that only one or the other response to losses has to be followed consistently by a manager. Although there are strategies that demand automatic actions after gains or losses of given magnitudes (i.e., "down 10 percent and out we go"), most managers approach losses on a case-by-case basis. They base their judgments on the circumstances of each situation and may sell one loss position and buy more of another.

The worst pattern would obviously be that of buying more of those stocks that then drop further and selling those that proceed to rise. Continual bad judgment like this will certainly reveal itself in disappointing total porfolio results over time. One pattern, not quite so apparent to the casual observer, is that of procrastination. For example, one mutual fund glorified its perception of a renaissance of the U.S. steel industry in its 1977 annual report. The fund had over 10 percent of its holdings in this industry, and management waxed eloquent over the wisdom of this decision. Twelve months later, conditions were decidedly worsening for steel, and by 24 months the fundamentals were weakening further. What was the response from the fund? In a word: nothing! No mention of the change and, most important, *no* reduction of steel stocks. A year or so later, with the industry now in poor shape, the steel holdings were identical to those of 1977 and 1978; they no longer constituted over 10 percent of the portfolio, but only because their market prices had dropped sharply (especially relative to the general market).

A "hear no evil, see no evil" portfolio approach suggests either: (1) a weak ownership conviction (probably about other holdings in the portfolio, too); (2) inertia; or (3) lack of attention to the account. Certainly these three tendencies have to be cardinal sins of money management.

Gains can be assessed in a similar manner. Is the manager unable to let anything positive last for long (in which case you had better be comfortable with a trading philosophy that may preclude ever realizing big individual security gains)? Does he consistently fail to take profits, generally staying so long that they are lost? Or do stocks simply remain in the portfolio and languish? The signs you are looking for—stubbornness, inertia, degree of flexibility, attention to the account—are as useful in studying gains as losses. Both provide valuable insights into manager qualities.

CONCLUSIONS

Once you have hired a manager, you have an opportunity to "live with" him. If you're like the husband who spends most of his time away from home, you will learn little about your manager and you will be prone to make shallow judgments. The grass will tend to look greener elsewhere, especially during the first dry spell, and you will be vulnerable to costly mistakes that shallow judgments generally produce. Yes, to assess whether your manager is one to "love" (i.e., competent), you must make an effort to know him. And to do this demands the kind of analysis that the general approaches and the specific Client Guides and Manager Queries of this book provide. If you believe that good results come from good relationships, you owe it to yourself—and to your money—to put these suggestions to work.

14

MAKING THE MOST OF MEETINGS

One of the better methods of forming good qualitative judgments of managers is to conduct efficient, penetrating, and meaningful manager meetings—far more efficient, penetrating, and meaningful than those that clients are conducting today. The meetings need not be frequent; in fact, if they occur too often,* they can take managers away from the investing they are paid handsomely to do.

Following are constructive thoughts and suggestions to improve client/manager meetings:

1.   It should be clear many weeks before the planned session *whose agenda is to be followed.* Inputs should come from both sides, but there should be an agenda.

2.   Each side should provide the other with relevant documentation many days before the meeting, so that sufficient time is allowed to digest important information.

3.   Each side should communicate by telephone at least a few days before the session to clear up any misunderstandings or to fill in any information voids.

4.   You should make sure that any performance analyses, either done in-house or obtained from consultants, are sent to your manager well before the personal meeting. Your manager should be able to contact the person(s) responsible for such analyses in plenty of time to arrive prepared to refute any figures or interpretations implied in these studies. There are too many occasions where managers are summarily presented with confusing analyses in front of a large group of client representatives; the combined pressures on the manager of inadequate knowledge of the analysis and inadequate meeting time amount to unfair conditions. One West Coast manager had just such an experience. Without warning, he was presented with a performance study that concluded that he had done very poorly for the client—whereas his figures showed reasonably decent

---

*The vast majority of clients, managers, and consultants agree that quarterly meetings are too frequent. Semiannual is now considered more normal; and in many cases, especially where good reporting exists and/or where the manager is well enough known to the client, annual get-togethers (well planned) are adequate.

returns on both an absolute and relative basis. "You can imagine my embarrassment and the impossibility of the situation," he complained to me.

> There were 14 people from the client company sitting at a boardroom table the size of a football field. The chairman of the board and the president were present, and each one was obviously anxious to proceed to what they considered more important matters than my outlook for the economy and my explanation of the existing portfolio of stocks and bonds. One other director had made it clear that he was to start vacation that afternoon. Another individual was dozing off for most of the session, and another was blowing cigar smoke in my face. With that atmosphere, I was expected to respond intelligently to something completely new to me and something very complicated mathematically. All I could think of was getting out of there, so I made an attempt at humor by stating that even General George Custer could look for troop replacements when he was surrounded by Indians. That broke the ice sufficiently for me to exit (and to hurry a response back to the company). But I can tell you that it was one hell of a way for any client to treat any manager, and I've lost plenty of sleep thinking about it since then.

5.   Other than sensible performance review, some worthwhile topics for good client/manager meetings include:

> a.   Review of the portfolio compared to your stated objectives. This should be used to reconfirm risk-taking tolerances and to confirm that no investment actions contrary to your instructions have been taken.

> *Manager Query: How do you understand our objectives and specific limitations (if any), and how are you conforming to these?*

> b.   Reiteration of your manager's investment style, so that you know what to expect under various circumstances. If you employ numerous managers, be sure to repeat any specific missions for which the manager present has been hired. If, for example, firm A is the only one employed for small-capitalization growth stock investing, it's a good idea to reiterate this fact and communicate how much of your portfolio is represented by this strategy.

Manager Query: Please restate your investment style and relate this to recent conditions within the marketplace. Show us how you are following or deviating from this style.

c.   Discussion of the investment manager's organization, with particular emphasis on what has changed. Questions on new account activity, size of assets under management, employee turnover, and compensation levels (as detailed in the Manager Queries, Client Guides, and other suggestions in prior chapters) should be a regular part of personal meetings.

d.   Manager presentation of economic, interest rate, and other forecasts. These can help you determine the scope of your management organization. This is not to say that good managers have to be accurate in this kind of forecasting. Some investors concentrate only on "bottom-up" stock selection and deemphasize top-down economic work. A manager who insists that a top-down perspective is important and who fails to exhibit much expertise in projecting economic trends is bound to be suspect, however.

e.   Listing of those securities with the largest gains and losses in the portfolio. This can provide a clue to manager style and to account supervision and attention. However, heavy concentration on existing losses has its limitations—and it can be destructive. As Bob Kirby (Capital Guardian) pointed out so aptly: "You don't have to have a very high I.Q. to figure out that if you simply sell the damn things, they won't be in the portfolio anymore and you won't have to flinch under the client's rubber hose every quarter." Instead of concentrating only on what went wrong, the kind of analysis covered in Client Guide 12 is recommended.

f.   Attention to portfolio structure, along with planned manager strategies.

g.   Review of quality ratings, average maturities, and marketability of any bonds under management.

h.   *Frank discussion of anything of special interest to either side, particularly any topic of importance to future investing policies*

*and anything that might have a bearing on future relationships
between the two of you.*

Not all of these suggested topics need be a part of a regular session. If
you are an institutional client, many review items might best be handled
through a client subcommittee meeting; conclusions could then be reported to a full complement of the committee *with the manager present.*
Furthermore, minutes of the meeting—generally taken by the client—
can add continuity and interest to future meetings. Copies of these
minutes should be mailed to your manager to complete the communication circle.

Minutes, however, seldom go beyond a mere reporting of whatever
the manager has chosen to discuss. A more useful assessment tool is *a
client log, designed to record specific questions and responses at regular
intervals, with important topics constantly tracked and updated.*

Please do not shudder at the suggestion of a meeting log. As organized
as you might be, I know that the thought of more paper and documentation is hardly pleasurable. But a log that serves to refresh your mind on
what a manager has said during meetings—even informal ones—can do
wonders for long-term assessment. I remember well how a most astute
international investor—the late Ronald Carnegie of Investors Capital of
Edinburgh, Scotland—kept and utilized a most efficient and useful filing
system. When I first met Carnegie in the mid-1960s, I specifically recommended that he consider owning the stock of Raychem Corporation of
Palo Alto, California. At that time, Raychem was in its formative stages
and was virtually unknown to domestic investors, much less to those
overseas.

I didn't know exactly how Carnegie treated this recommendation until
3 or 4 years later when I visited him again. In the course of conversation,
Carnegie inquired how I felt about Raychem. When I told him, he asked
for my patience while he went to his files, and he leafed to a page that told
him exactly what I had suggested to him about the stock 3 or 4 years
earlier. He had liked the idea originally, based mainly on my view of the
company's strategic strengths within new fields of polymers and heat-
shrinkable products; his renewed questioning was intended to determine

whether the considerations had been correct and whether he should now reevaluate them. In short, he had a better picture of my judgment than perhaps even my own memory provided. Carnegie was a successful investor, and his associates in Edinburgh will tell you that his filing system was integral to his good judgment of others.

Memories can be short, and an efficient paper trail can overcome even extreme forgetfulness. *A client log will prepare you well for both ensuing meetings and sound manager assessment.*

For example, you should keep a log on personnel changes within your money manager's organization. No meeting should end without your:

> ***Manager Query:***   *What personnel changes have occurred in your firm since our last meeting?*

You may or may not care who sweeps up at good old ABC Capital Management, but you should care about key personnel (including back-ups and promising young people). Major defections can radically alter the future performance prospects of a firm. A series of less major defections may indicate that larger problems are brewing.

A log should also include the following:

1.   Manager forecasts plotted against what actually occurred
2.   A survey of market strategies proposed, with information as to how they were carried out
3.   Business and other information about your manager, derived from the following:

> ***Manager Queries:***   *How many accounts have been added or lost? What is the size of assets under your management? How well has our account performed relative to other accounts of your firm?*

Any additional points of client interest—including many of the items suggested in Chapters 10 through 12—should also be tracked. Following is a sample log (Client Guide 13) that should help you organize your own

CLIENT GUIDE 13
Client Log of Manager Meetings

Manager Org.:   Manager Representative:

Date:

Our Group Present: Absent:

I. Manager Organization Info:

                                        Current   19__   19__   19__

Mgr. Assets under management

                    Fixed income

                    Equities

                    Other (   )

                    Total

          Pertinent comments:

Comparison, manager's composite performance vs. our account and vs. our chosen Index(es):

                                          Current   19__   19__   19__

(Their composite)   Fixed income

                        Our account

                        Chosen index

      (Composite)   Equities

                        Our account

                        Chosen index

      (Composite)   Other (   )

                        Our account

                        Chosen index

      (Composite)   Balanced account

                        Our account

                        Chosen index

        Pertinent comments:

      Annualized cumulative performance:

                        2 yrs   3 yrs   4 yrs   5 yrs   6 yrs   7 yrs   Inception

Fixed income

(composite)

Our account

Index

Equities

(composite)

Our account

Index

	2 yrs	3 yrs	4 yrs	5 yrs	6 yrs	7 yrs	Inception

Other
(composite)
Our account
Index
Balanced
(composite)
Our account
Index

Manager number of client account relationships:

	Current	19__	19__	19__
Fixed income				
Equities				
Other ( )				
Total				

Manager personnel   Current   19__   19__   19__
    Number of principals:
    Number of employees:
    Research personnel:
    Portfolio management
    Pertinent comments:

II.   Manager's own statement of his style, with any particulars relating to present cycles:

III.   Manager's specific forecasts:
    Macro (economy, interest rates, inflation, corporate profitability, currencies, etc.):

    Strategies:
      Re industries
        individual companies
        portfolio structure

IV.   Our portfolio observations:
      His handling of: gains
              losses

V.   General discussion:

VI.   Pending matters:

records of manager meetings. Your discipline in recording manager meetings can lead only to better judgments of whether "to keep or not to keep."

CONCLUSIONS

Client/manager meetings should exist to protect both parties. Properly conducted, they set the stage for efficient qualitative assessment of managers not available other ways. Working sessions should not be overly polite; items that need to be discussed should surface early, and appropriate time should be devoted to them. Mainly, the meetings should ensure that your objectives and your manager understandings are in sync—and that the manager you hired has essentially the same talents, motivation, and wherewithal you originally trusted. If you are an institutional client, the meetings should allow *as many of your group as possible to form sound qualitative judgments of the managers all of you have chosen*—and a well-designed log of manager meetings should help you objectively assess their qualities and performance over the long term.

15

MANAGING YOUR MANAGER— ANOTHER WAY TO ACHIEVE HIGHER INVESTMENT RETURNS

If you can keep your head when all
about you are losing theirs . . .
Rudyard Kipling
If

In working with a manager, sound guidelines, clear objectives, and good client meetings are obviously only part of a successful approach. If consistent follow-through doesn't exist, then all this work becomes like the proverbial road to hell that is paved with good intentions.

For example, such intentions can be rendered meaningless by ensuing verbal communcations between you and your manager. The most casual comments can interfere with the cooperative client/manager association that is most conducive to superior investment results.

You need not be devious or unreasonable to send out strange signals to your manager. Clients' very human tendencies to vacillate slightly or to hedge instructions can lead to surprisingly detrimental manager behavior. Take a seemingly harmless client statement like "We're in this for a full market cycle, but we'd like to get the best returns we can in the interim." It *could* create doubt in a manager's mind about the formal client statement that "short-term, interim investment results are entirely secondary to realistic longer-term goals." While you might only be verbalizing a hope, not a demand, your "we'd like to get the best returns we can in the interim" *might* create doubts about your patience. Furthermore, the plea for "best returns" is made without reference to acceptable risk parameters. Many managers are sensitive to (*probably paranoid about*) client intimations that good results had better show up fairly quickly. Hence, very innocent statements can create doubts as to whether your written and reiterated guidelines have real meaning.

Whenever confusion emerges, it can affect investment policy in a way not anticipated by either party. You think you have exhibited reasonableness, yet your manager picks out the "best returns" as a strong challenge to go beyond your lower-risk dictum. Wars are caused by smaller misunderstandings!

Danger exists any time you and your manager "talk around" an important subject and fail to reach a mutual understanding. The most serious confusion occurs when there is no agreement about whether maximum downside protection or upside participation should predominate. Remember: You cannot demand both.

Another mistake is made when one person in a client organization tries to invoke *personal* investment idiosyncrasies that differ from his organization's written objectives. One client representative is known in investment manager circles for vociferously preaching his personal preference for market timing, despite the fact that his company seems ill suited to an active trading strategy. As a result, his managers—most of whom are doubters about this investment style—are probably more tentative in carrying out their best strategies and have to be virtual "iron men" to resist pleasing this one individual.

Another client is reputed to foster manager confusion by constantly reminding his hirees that his number one objective is limited downside— yet he consistently tells his managers what a screaming buy he considers the market to be. *He* may feel covered both ways, but his managers apparently feel damned if they do and damned if they don't!

If managers are compromised by vagueness or confusion or inconsistency, why don't they demand clearer definitions? Aside from Chapter 4's explanation that they *may* have little to lose by taking the account,* the most important reasons for manager acquiescence are the following:

1.   They doubt that consistent conclusions can be reached anyway.
2.   They certainly want to avoid controversy with the people who are paying their bills.
3.   They consider it risky to be conservative (realistic) about how much of a return a client should expect from investment markets and how soon; they prefer not to reduce client confidence in their abilities, *particularly since they know that there are countless managers who will intimate or promise greater and quicker successes.*
4.   They are fearful of contradicting or disappointing clients at the same time that they are imposing on their valuable time.

Hence, the mixed signals continue—and with them, the diminished chances for a successful client/manager relationship. Following are

---

*If they are exceptional managers, this is very shortsighted, as business will eventually come their way and they should avoid the disruptions that poor client relationships involve.

some important examples of the kind of confusion that can evolve from some typical, and in most cases innocent, client dicta. Client Guide 14 lists some common client statements (column 1) and common interpretations of these statements by managers (column 2), followed by the likely manager investment response (column 3), along with general comments and suggestions for both parties (column 4). Chances are that you or your associates have made at least one of the dicta, so you should understand the practical consequences of what may have been casual remarks. (Since an "ideal" suggested dictum has been included, there is reason for *all* readers to follow the Guide.)

The major intent of this Guide is to create greater *empathy* on both sides of the client/manager team. *Realistic investment expectations should be confirmed by realistic future statements and behavior.*

SECOND-GUESSING

Not included among the dicta is another very normal and generally harmful human tendency: *second-guessing*. If you want to participate in the management of your account, you can either withhold full discretion and relegate the account to an "advisory" status or plan to interfere only where you have some special insights that might be helpful to the account. The trouble with nondiscretionary accounts is that most of the better managers won't take them; and, even if they do, you risk not getting their full talents. The trouble with your interfering, even with "special insights," is that you will be deciding which insights are indeed "special." Do you really have something unique to add to the process? Can you make such a judgment? Aren't you simply diffusing your agent's know-how? Furthermore, second-guessing regularly in any account is bound to be disruptive. Raised eyebrows, innuendos, or blatant "I told you so's" can produce a "hybrid" portfolio, with securities held or avoided because of your manager's perception of what will make you happiest or unhappiest. While managers may not admit to this kind of fear or obsequiousness, portfolio structures can be heavily influenced this way— normally to the ultimate, and often serious, detriment of performance.

CLIENT GUIDE 14
Confusing Client Dicta

(1) Possible Client Dictum	(2) Which the Manager Generally Interprets as Meaning	(3) And Which Often Produces This Manager Response	(4) General Comment
"Get me the best returns over a market cycle."	The source of returns will not be as important as the results. Top quartile performance may be required over *all* cycles.	Take greater risks—less emphasis on diversification.	Can you (the client) really afford the risks? Are you expecting the best of all worlds? Suggested improvement: Discuss the amount of risk to be assumed.
"*Absolute* returns are our goal. (I can't 'eat' relative returns!)"	Client is willing to give up some upside for downside protection and consistency. Relative judgments less important.	Less risk taking. More diversification. More cash (perhaps more market timing).	Will you be satisfied with mediocre returns in ebullient periods? Suggested improvement: Confirm that relative performance will not influence you significantly.

(1)	(2)	(3)	(4)
	Which the Manager Generally Interprets as Meaning	And Which Often Produces This Manager Response	
Possible Client Dictum			General Comment
"My goals are *real* (above inflation) returns."	Client expects markets to reflect inflation—so just keep ahead of it by some predetermined amount.	Probably have to use lots of market timing/cash, because there's normally a lag between inflation and market reactions.	Will you wait long enough for the lags to be overcome? Example of 1973 and 1974, which produced negative real returns of 60 to 70%. Do you have the patience? Suggested improvement: Agree that real goals require considerable time for assessment—i.e., minimum of 5 years plus adjustments for the 1973–1974 type of "real" upsets.
"Don't bother me with definitions. Do the best you can."	Client is likely to shift goals from relative to absolute to who-knows-what. Also means that client is either so "fat" that he can absorb any shortfalls or does not want to define himself.	Give it your "best shot," but with fear of inconsistent client risk posture. Confusion about client goals creates a queasiness about a long-term relationship with manager.	Are you really willing to let your managers decide your fate? Suggested improvement: You and your manager must work hard to be more specific. Still, the responsibility belongs to you, the client.

We'll judge you relative to the respective markets."

Manager's equities versus S&P 500; bonds versus some intermediate-maturity bond index. Both relative to other managers and both additionally adjusted for style and for risk assumed.

May worry about being un-invested in any area of sig-nificance (if so, mediocrity becomes the goal). May also follow big trends (i.e., 30% in energy stocks in 1980; or, in bonds, large percentages in cash equivalents vs. other maturity bonds).

Probe to determine which is more important—making money or avoiding large de-clines.
Follow suggestions and for-mat of Chapter 3.

Relative goals assume all markets you're in will pro-duce required absolute obli-gations. Relatives do provide judgment of your manager, but there may be better bogeys.

Suggested improvement:
Be more specific about de-sires for results in ebullient, normal, or very poor mar-kets. As with all of the above, be more specific about your time horizon and about your not simply casting about for other managers who may (will) look better periodically.

(1)	(2)	(3)	(4)
Possible Client Dictum	Which the Manager Generally Interprets as Meaning	And Which Often Produces This Manager Response	General Comment
"Our quantitative *and* qualitative judgments of ourselves lead us to believe that we are most vulnerable to . . . (set of economic conditions) plus our risk posture is . . . ; we *are* willing to look out 5 to 10 years for returns from various assets and look at least 5 years for quantitative assessment of our managers (qualitative going on all the time).	No "home runs" demanded; need solid returns over time, with our risk taking adequately defined.	Can spend time on investment decisions. Can manage account within a logical set of objectives.	Both parties at least working from a "relaxed," well-thought-out posture. Performance results are generally superior under such conditions. Suggested improvement: None.

Actually, the intent of second-guessing may not necessarily be to influence portfolio strategy. The manager, on the other hand, has trouble distinguishing harmlessly intended doubting from threatening negative suggestions. Either way, the result is manager uncertainty, not a trait conducive to great decision making. If you have decided to seek competent outside help, it is logical to assume that you want the chosen manager's best shot, which a portfolio influenced by your biases is not going to represent.

Take the case of two brothers who were clients of one management firm. Each brother had his own portfolio—both were inherited and contained identical securities. Brother A was relaxed and never interfered with decisions, while brother B concerned himself with what was owned and why. A truly gave full discretion, while B gave contractual discretion that was muted by his interference. Performance results began deviating almost from the start for the two accounts. After the first few years, what had been identical $2 million portfolios were separated by about $300,000 (A over B). After 4 years, $1 million more rested in A than in B. And within 6 years, A's assets were double those of B. Another manager might have been immune to the suggestions and the second-guessing of B, but it takes someone very strong and very opinionated to resist the will of the person paying the fees. Countless situations such as this exist, and in most cases the interfering, second-guessing client underperforms those who instill confidence and give good managers full latitude to make decisions.

This is not to imply that full discretion can be given by every client or is deserved by every manager. Yet one thing is certain: Inconsistent portfolio structuring—which comes from managers owning securities about which they are hesitant—makes for less efficient investment management.

One sensible suggestion is for you to entrust money only to those in whom you have sufficient confidence to give control. If you cannot bring yourself to do this with total assets, then carve out that portion you are willing to relinquish to full discretion and then channel another portion for your own or other management. Unless you are very unsuccessful with the latter, the chances are good that the two separately managed funds will do better than one you cannot "let go."

HANDLING ANGER

Both you and your manager should control the anger that might erupt after disappointing results. Managers often respond by eliminating the disappointing, losing securities. Strange as it may seem, there are managers who admit knowing at the very time they're disposing of such an investment that they should be *buying,* not selling—but they cannot stop themselves. The very best managers overcome this and act opposite to the way their frustration seems to prompt, but even the best occasionally fall victim to such reactions. It took an honest professional like Barton Biggs to write, "In the past, I have found that selling a few good stocks for no good reason other than that you can't take the punishment anymore usually will turn the market."

Clients often vent such anger by firing the manager whose short-term performance is trying them. The best clients, like the best managers, do not follow the easy path to erase the source of disappointment; instead they follow the unconventional but sound approach to inevitable "glitches" of adding to their holdings (at obviously depressed prices) by giving more funds to the lagging managers who pass the qualitative tests emphasized in this book.

MORE ON THE PROPER "CARE AND FEEDING" OF MONEY MANAGERS

The best personal relationships are two-way, and your client/manager duo is no exception. You should expect good service from your manager, but you must reciprocate with similar efforts. If you neglect this, you not only will reduce your chances for deriving the maximum from your managers, but you also may not even be able to attract the best managers (since many of the smartest managers simply avoid associations with problem clients). Your client responsibilities are wide and varied; they range from good communications to what one might call "issuing proper rewards and punishment."

As mentioned, few investment managers respond favorably to "produce or else" demands. Like other people, portfolio managers are likely to strain under too much pressure, especially since they are already exposed to the never-ending tensions of the financial markets. Remember, bond and stock market values appear as if in fishbowls; the fact that prices appear daily is an indication of marketability, but the same day-to-day fluctuations create potential psychological problems, too. While managers are paid handsomely to operate efficiently under such tensions, this hardly guarantees success. It takes fortitude and conviction to buy and sell securities well, especially during difficult cycles and style trends. Actions by you that imply lack of confidence in your manager or hint of impatience are likely to inhibit the very skills you are hiring. Be careful not to emphasize what manager Mitch Milias calls "the four W's: "What went wrong with ———!"

It may sound Pollyanna-ish, but encouragement can help a lot—*intelligent encouragement, that is.* This means *encouragement without overraction, in both positive and negative environments.*

When things are going famously, of course be complimentary and appreciative. But do not become so carried away that you hand the top performers the keys to your store. Booms in specialized investment styles have, over and over again, tempted clients to play a follow-the-leader tack that has usually led to investing disappointments.

It's an old Wall Street adage that "trees don't grow to the sky," which means that individual stocks, industry groups, and investment styles do not rise forever. Dramatic manager overperformance seldom lasts forever, either, which means that you should be wary of apparent manager dominance. Certainly you should not throw huge amounts of money at a style that has been very popular for a few years or more.

Similarly, you should approach poor near-term performance with a tolerant, mature attitude. Make sure you do not instill in your manager excessive worry about failing. The famous high-wire acrobat, Karl Wallenda, was a man of steel nerves and maximum proficiency until he shifted his focus toward *not falling.* He fell to his death shortly thereafter. *If your qualitative judgment of a manager firm remains the same as when you retained it,* do not look down your nose. The manager's investing style is probably temporarily unpopular. As Boeing's overseer of pension assets, Gary Bland, remarks: "Good investment people simply don't turn stupid!"

SHOULD YOU GIVE MORE FUNDS TO AN UNDERPERFORMING MANAGER?

A number of studies—and numerous experts—suggest exactly this. Earlier, George Russell and Barton Biggs were quoted as recommending contrarian strategies of money flows to managers. A 1983 *Journal of Portfolio Management* article[*] confirmed this by showing how clients would have fared so much better from 1973 through 1982 by shifting away from the top performers. Starting with 3-year records from 1973 through 1975, the authors found only 5 percent of the first-quartile managers persisting in the subsequent 3 years—while 40 percent of the fourth-quartile portfolios moved to the top quartile. The dramatic shifts in investment styles depicted in Chapter 5 suggested similar patterns from 1968 right on through the present.

Heretical as it may sound, there *are* strong reasons to consider giving *more* money to *certain* performance laggards. The most obvious reason is that the manager whose stocks are out of favor *may now own cheap, underpriced stocks.* If true, you may be getting less risk, more value, and more ultimate upside potential—perhaps way more than the securities held by the current superstar managers.

You should take courage from knowing that at least 75 percent and perhaps as many as 95 percent of investor clients reward managers "on a roll." You should also take courage from Figure 2.1 which depicts how perfectly atrocious the timing of pension fund cash flows into common stocks has been over the past 28 years.

Of course, you don't want to throw good money after bad managers. In

---

[*]Patricia C. Dunn and Rolf D. Theisen, "How Consistently Do Active Managers Win?" Summer, 1983.

this case "bad" managers are those who have inferior judgment or show insensitivity to client needs and objectives—not those who turn in a poor but understandable near-term performance. Success will follow only where managerial *qualities* excel (the tools for making sound qualitative judgments have been provided) *and where you can understand the reasons for underperformance*. By making the effort to assess the qualities and to fit the trends to certain identifiable styles and managers, you can position yourself on the most reliable and productive road to success.

One word of caution: Do not jump into such contrary cash direction policies where styles have been *very* widely embraced by investors. The Nifty Fifty mania that culminated in 1972 and 1973 and the energy stock surge that ended in 1980 left institutional (and other) accounts so loaded with these stocks (over 30 percent of most portfolios) that a long and painful disgorgement process was inevitable. Jumping back too soon into manager organizations rigidly committed to these securities would have been a mistake. So judgment is required. Still, the strategy of leaning against broad investor popularity is sound.

PATIENCE

Patience is a required virtue for most successful investing. The principle "Those who cannot wait never win" normally prevails.

Similarly, there is a periodic need for tolerance of good managers caught in a sound but currently unpopular philosophy. The client with an itchy trigger finger usually finds himself involved in unproductive hassles, with transaction and execution costs eating away at capital.

Dean LeBaron chides clients for the negative impact they have on their own performance by foolishly emphasizing short-term results. The net effect, LeBaron argues, is that clients "are likely to encourage higher turnover rates." Walter Cabot, the president of the Harvard Management Company, the investment subsidiary that runs the university's endowment, believes that "there's a conflict between short-term and long-term investing. The more you chase the Holy Grail of short-term performance, the less you get in long-term results." Despite such advice, clients are still tempted to dismiss managers arbitrarily if their account suffers 2 poor years in a row. *The disappointment may be deserved, but the response is generally costly.* You shouldn't act in concert with our "Endless Circle of Clients Zigging While Cycles Are Zagging" (Client Guide 5). That advice is echoed by the experience of many publicly traded mutual funds, including some with vastly superior long-term records, such as Investment Company of America, Templeton Growth, and Wellington. These three, along with other mutuals and many fine organizations whose records are not publicly traded (but available), have all had instances of 2 poor relative years *that have been followed immediately by a number of powerful overperforming years.*

Client impatience has other negative ramifications. The nervousness it creates in managers often causes *corporate* officials to run their businesses less sensibly. Jean Riboud, chairman of Schlumberger, Ltd., described this insidious temptation in a June 13, 1983, *New Yorker* magazine interview. Riboud claimed that short-term stock market pressures only interfere with management's major responsibilty, which is for longer-term performance. He stated that "one of the things wrong with American industry is its preoccupation with quarterly statements." Ed Littlefield, former chairman of another fine company, Utah International (subsequently merged into G.E.), told a Stanford Business School advisory group in 1983 that he found it more efficient to manage Utah as a private rather than a public company "because [he] could make more intelligent business decisions when the horizon was longer." Littlefield acknowledged that he once made a decision as a public company that he knew would have short-term negative implications on his stock but that was right for his company in the long term. Despite his conviction, Littlefield indicated that the market's reactions "were such that [he] thought long and hard before he would duplicate such a decision." Hence, clients can affect businesses through the instrument of their managers. This highlights the patience question—that is, *do you really want a manager who emphasizes companies that concentrate on the expedient rather than the wisest decisions?* Your response might be that the manager mission is coldly to produce investment results—so to heck with idealism. A legitimate response would be: *Isn't this manager's approach,*

*consciously or subconsiously encouraged by the client, simply intro-
ducing more risk into the portfolio?*

You can see the vicious cycle this produces—just another negative
concentration on near-term performance numbers. It's not only detrimental to results but also injurious to our country's economic system.
First Boston's Al Wojnilower foresees dire consequences from excessive
financial maneuvering, including overly active clients. In an October 30,
1981, speech, Wojnilower stated that "switching around pension fund
managers in search of above-average performance" is "no different from
gambling, and the dangers to innocent bystanders and posterity are
greater." Wojnilower fears that "the financial community has largely lost
its ability to maintain the imperatives of order, continuity and triviality
that human institutions must satisfy in order to survive." As sophisticated
as American businesspeople, educators, and the like can be in some
areas, it is appalling how amateurish they can be when overseeing investment portfolios.

BUT DON'T YOU HAVE A RIGHT TO CRITICIZE YOUR MANAGERS?

The advantage of *encouraging* good managers is not meant to rule out
discouragement on your part as a client. After all, the money *is* yours;
losses and relative underperformance are not to be cheered; and managers often deserve to be fired. You simply have to be careful not to fall into
the trap of what Nobel prize winner (1977) Herbert Simon calls "bounded
rationality"—a way of describing how people muddle through a world of
baffling complexity. Simon argues that humans have a *perverse* tendency
to let feelings overcome logic. Thus, it is very important to learn when to
praise and when to grumble with good reason, to learn how to attain the
happy medium between naive encouragement and detrimental
discouragement.

The answer, again, is not to overreact to either exceptionally good
news or bad; instead, you should aim to make dispassionate judgments
of managers and to lean toward encouragement wherever possible.

HOW LONG SHOULD YOU WAIT BEFORE MAKING JUDGMENTS?

There is no sacrosanct time period in which to make proper manager assessments. Broad markets have varying spans of volatility, as do particular investing styles. Still, you have to decide how long to wait for the fruits of your manager selections. Three years is widely considered to be a minimum period for proper assessment, provided of course that manager qualities (the people and their attention to their business) remain intact. Other clients recognize how shortsighted a 3-year view can be and settle on a "full market cycle." This is unfortunately vague; a full market cycle can be anything, including a period of much less than 3 years. Others compromise on a 3- to 5-year goal.

If clients had proper patience and if managers remained as they were qualitatively, the most productive approach would be to assess over a minimum of 5 years. The fact of life is that "Stay as sweet as you are and we won't leave you for 5 to 10 years" is a difficult promise for most to keep. The anomaly is that bond and stock managers are seldom hired with such long-range scope, and yet venture capital, real estate, and, recently, leveraged buyout funds are granted just such (5- or 10- or even 12-year) contracts. One might conjecture that results from venture capital and real estate have been particularly favorable because, among other reasons, investors have been forced into long-term assessments. Managers of these other assets surely benefit from being given more time and from feeling less client pressures.

The best approach, therefore, is to consider any assessment time frame as approximate and to concentrate on the quantitative and qualitative techniques offered in this book—constantly restraining yourself from indulging those natural human tendencies that promote hyperactivity, impatience, and follow-the-leader behavior, all of which interfere with good investing.

CONCLUSIONS

Life can be terribly difficult for people without money. While few of those with capital would trade places with those without, having money nevertheless creates complications of its own. A very wealthy man once wisely remarked: "Things were certainly simpler when I didn't have a dime!"

Whether the money is your own or whether you are involved in overseeing monetary affairs of others, making the funds for which you are responsible grow creates its own set of obligations. Some of these obligations can be fulfilled by building good client/manager relationships.

While managers have a big role to play in such relationships, you must understand how important it will be to your long-term interests *to cultivate your managers just as assiduously as the managers cultivate you*. The adage "The customer is always right" doesn't always apply to the personal service business—and it certainly does not pertain to money management.

Be careful not to take the expression "managing your manager" literally. There is a big difference between good monitoring and a managing process that emphasizes interference. You should indeed "manage" your overall risk taking through good investment guidelines and intelligent asset mix. But you should avoid interfering with the tactical decisions at which your manager should be skilled.

You needn't coddle your manager, but you can shape a certain amount of your performance destiny through reasonable patience, understanding, intelligent encouragement, and the fortitude to fight the herd instinct. While this attitude by itself cannot ensure investment success—for example, it won't help you if you choose *inferior* managers—the "right" approach with the right managers enhances the probabilities for investment happiness. As one noted investment manager said: "Client does as client is!" Or "Client prospers as client acts." The challenge is made difficult because it requires calm, reasonableness, tolerance, and patience during the occasional and inevitable trying investment times. Kipling's *If* says it all: "If—you can keep your head when all about you are losing theirs. . . ."

16

GRABBING THE GOLD RING

Success is that old ABC—ability,
breaks, and courage.

> Charles Luckman
> *New York Mirror*
> September 19, 1955

While pure, unadulterated luck plays a heavy role in life, most very successful people make their own breaks by combining the courage of their convictions with their abilities, which in turn have benefited from *good preparation*. In time, the masters of most trades bother less and less with intricate details, relying more and more on a perceptiveness that combines good sense with the most important considerations.

The same is true of successful investors. Many of the most proficient common stock investors, for example, are not necessarily adept at knowing all the details of the companies they own. They gather sufficient knowledge of the businesses these companies are engaged in and how they are managed and then combine their "feeling for quality" with a value judgment of these securities relative to others in the marketplace. They then juggle all of this in their minds to make superior *final judgments*. It is the genius of this juggling process—their intuition or perceptiveness—that separates most superb investors from the pack.

Judging investment managers requires a similar juggling process. The intent of the past 15 chapters has been to provide a wealth of knowledge for you to absorb, to help you develop a *strong client perceptiveness*. You will never have the time to ask all the questions or to know all there is to know about the managers you assess, but you now have the background, sophistication, and thought process that should lead to sound decisions. Your practical understanding of investing, of the investment management business, of efficient people and organization assessment, and of the important do's and don'ts of investor/manager relationships is enough to keep you from being badly fooled—and to produce an excellent instinct that should lead you to the selection and retention of superior manager talent.

The steps are simple enough. First, understand your own or your organization's investment needs and personality. Have the potential manager assess his investing characteristics too, then make sure the profiles complement instead of clash with each other. Set clear, practical objectives—and make sure that ensuing verbal instructions do not contradict them! Understand enough about market cycles and styles to recognize where manager performance bonanzas are not likely to recur.

Remind yourself how luck can play a big role in investment results. Try to distinguish true investing wisdom from the "gifts" of fortune.

Look beyond fancy presentations to discern the actual capabilities of the management firms you're assessing—and strive to see behind the deceptive veil of performance numbers. Demand composite performance records of *every* dollar managed. Choose carefully those periods on which you base your assessment of investment managers in order to avoid potentially misleading "magic periods." Understand the special problems posed by balanced account reporting—and make sure that a proper assessment of risk is included in your manager's (or prospective manager's) communications.

Define your manager's investment philosophy—including its implications—and then check to see that it matches his actions. Analyze the management firm's personnel strengths and weaknesses, as well as its ability to hire and retain good people And understand the subtle messages that fee structures convey.

Client Guide 15 is a summary of some of the more important considerations for anyone planning to entrust funds to others. It should serve as a minimum checklist of items you should assess of those individuals or organizations who purport to invest your money wisely. The very least you should expect from managers is shown in Client Guide 15 on the next page. Most of the information can be supplied to you prior to any personal meetings.* Certain manager responses may lead to further questions, many of which again can be handled prior to formalized meetings. It is important to cover the basics in a way that leaves room for incisive qualitative probing when you conduct your personal interviewing. To repeat a statement made earlier, make sure that *you* control the important interviews and that you are not intimidated by fancy slide shows, marketing presentations, or powerful individuals.

Once you have hired a manager, analyze why money has been made or lost in your account and how the manager reacts to failure or success.

---

*The exception is client references. You cannot expect a manager to supply these until your seriousness as a potential client has been well established.

CLIENT GUIDE 15
A Minimum Checklist For Manager Assessment

Characteristics of the investment manager firm

Investing background of the managers, as individuals and as a unit
Number and types of clients; total money under management; minimum and average account size
Operating experience with clients (accounts gained and lost over the years)
Investment capabilities, specializations, and voids
Broad investment philosophy and specific style
Any possible conflicts of interest with clients
Fees (and the "statement" they make)
Manager sources of information
Uniqueness: Where does it exist?

Specifics dealing with your account

Person(s) to be directly responsible for the management of your funds
A match of your investment objectives and communication needs with manager style and capabilities
Number of securities likely to be held in your account; and likely turnover of assets annually

Performance

Records presented: Are they all-inclusive and representative of all types of environments?
A match of the manager's past record with your objectives and the manager's stated risk taking and style
Any special circumstances affecting performance

Other

Client references (current and past)

Conduct efficient and productive meetings—and keep an organized account of what has been said as well as updates on personnel changes and other matters affecting the management of your portfolio. Avoid giving your manager mixed signals. Provide intelligent encouragement, criticism when necessary—and, above all, the patience to allow your manager to perform.

A FINAL CHALLENGE TO CLIENTS AND MANAGERS

As explained in Chapter 1, the investment management industry in its present form is very young; in its rapid change and growth, many excesses have developed. A polite way to put it would be that some constructive changes are in order; a more candid way of phrasing it would be that the industry needs to "clean up its act," just as clients and consultants need to improve their behavior.

How will progress emerge? Must we wait for the Securities and Exchange Commission or national legislation to institute some crucial changes? One would hope not, because of the politics that would doubtless interfere with ideal solutions, and because governmental agencies seldom have the staff, the funds, or perhaps even the true understanding of the business to handle the job well. Besides which, penalties meted by the S.E.C. (and industry self-regulating bodies) are too often light wrist taps that are inadequate disincentives to the potential violators. The media can help by publicizing questionable practices, but their efforts are most likely to fade into the night, provoking greater awareness without prompting specific solutions. Consultants could contribute more than they do to the solution, too, although in certain instances they constitute part of the problem and thus may not be the ideal ones to bring about appropriate changes.

So the burden for change definitely rests on the group that has the most to gain—*you, the clients*. If those of you who are entrusting money to others are to get what you desire, you had better shake the tree yourselves!

The starting point for you is to *get involved*. If you are a personal investor, you can demand what institutional investors receive—the same kind of attention, the same reporting methods and communication, including (at least from now on) honest performance data. If you represent an institution, push hard to heighten the involvement of your compatriots, including high-ranked executives and directors, who have the responsibility to raise their knowledge and sophistication, too. Attention should be given to the questionnaires presented earlier, along with other specific advice.

Larger client associations, including existing "splinter groups" of pension administrators and others, should start active programs demanding greater standardization of performance calculation and reporting. Establish a data bank of all the composite performance figures you should now be demanding from all managers. Be as harsh on your own methods, however, as you plan to be on those of the managers you are assessing. Do not do as one group of administrators has done: They have compiled statistics on managers presently hired, dropping from their compilation those no longer employed. By doing this, they have created an unrealistic moving target, not truly representative of actual experience.

Clients should also organize themselves to make better qualitative judgments, instituting numerous suggestions and formal procedures included in prior chapters. Efforts should also be made to probe consultants—to determine whether they in fact know managers as they say they do, to determine whether their performance comparisons are as accurate as they should be.

"Reform" in the investment management business should certainly not come only from client insistence. Most managers have considerable incentive to improve their industry standards, too. "Cleaning up" should also come from manager associations and societies—posthaste!

Managers should be less reluctant to push for realistic client guidelines and for responsible efforts to create the kind of team that produces best for both parties. What impact managers can have on clients is questionable. After all, the clients are the clients; it is hard for managers to point their fingers in criticism at the people who pay the bills. As Woody Allen says, "The lion shall lie down with the lamb, but the lamb won't get much sleep." While most of the advice and the Client Guides of this book are designed to help you see through the manager hype or simply make more rational appraisals of manager organizations, the relationship should be two-way. Managers should be able to comment on your guidelines without fear of retribution on the other side; they should expect greater consistency as a result of your own enhanced self-knowledge (which you can achieve through Client Guides 1 and 2). In other words, while it's difficult for managers to ask for "equal time," you should encourage manager feedback along with efforts to improve investment management industry standards.

Managers have a responsibility to be more professional. They should be more realistic about risk taking and about the things they can and cannot do well. They should manage their businesses better, including gaining better control over their trading costs. They should communicate better with clients. And, to repeat, they should do everything they can to force high standards and complete honesty on themselves and fellow investment managers.

Consultants should eliminate their shortcomings, too. Standards must be raised, and clients must be assured that only their best interests are at heart and in practice at all times.

The plea, therefore, goes out. "Revolutionists arise, wherever you are! If you care about yourself, about the investment industry, or simply about what's right versus what's wrong, your efforts for change are needed."

PULLING IT ALL TOGETHER

Nobody should promise you any rose gardens in the quest for superior investment management. Choices are not easy—and they never will be. But you can do the job far more successfully and effectively then others have in the past—particularly because your look into the inner sanctum of the investment management business has provided you with a solid defense against a vagary of deceptive practices.

The building blocks are there for the constructive team effort that fosters investment success. Your offense now consists of an imaginative approach to qualitative assessment of managers, a sensible view of risk, and numerous techniques for choosing the winners of the future. You are informed enough to be wary and knowledgeable enough to be astute. Your perceptiveness has been heightened, and you have enough specific props to aid your assessment process, now and in the future. In short, you know what to look for and what to look *out* for, which means that you should possess the skills to choose the investment management winners of the future and to be a superior client, too.

Worry no more about the Pied Piper! You are now able to achieve investment success under reasonable, comfortable conditions—and able to help create a healthier investing atmosphere for yourself, other clients, and well-intentioned, competent investment managers and consultants.

A SUMMARY OF CLIENT GUIDES

Following is a listing of the 15 Client Guides presented in this book—to be used in conjunction with other advice offered.

Client Guide Number	Page Reference	Value of the Client Guide
1	Ch 3 Pg 33	An easy-to-use "Know Your Investor Self" questionnaire to enable individuals and organizations to understand their financial character and their investment personalities. The starting point for investing comfortably and sensibly and for setting reasonable objectives.
2	Ch 3 Pgs 35–37	A more specific Client Investment Personality Questionnaire. An organized way to describe what you want from your investing and from an investment manager.
2a	Ch 3 Pgs 37–39	A mirror image of Client Guide 2, this is for prospective managers to complete. Matching this against Client Guide 2 will enable you to concentrate on those managers who complement you best.
3	Ch 4 Pgs 49–53	A model set of investment guidelines that serves as a checklist for your statement of clear and reasonable objectives.
4	Ch 5 Pgs 61–65	A "Statement of Manager Investment Style and Risk Taking"—another organized way to know what you're getting from a manager before you engage him. Also, an aid to analyzing past performance results.

Client Guide Number	Page Reference	Value of the Client Guide
5	Ch 5 Pg 20	The Rosenberg "Endless Circle of Client Zigging When Cycles Are Zagging"—a way to learn from the errors of others how to avoid typically unprofitable client actions and to time your investments better.
6	Ch 7 Pgs 100–101	A method for analyzing manager strategies and styles by tracking specific portfolio industry moves.
7	Ch 8 Pg 112	A Preferred report designed to allow you to assess the performance of bonds and stocks within a balanced account. This eliminates the weaknesses of today's standard reporting, which too often creates a deceptive picture of a manager's talents.
8	Ch 9 Pg 132	A very sensible way for you to judge the risks assumed in a fixed-income portfolio. With this comes a better way of judging performance.
8a	Ch 9 Pgs 133–134	The same as Client Guide 8, but for *equity* portfolio risk and performance measurement.
9	Ch 10 Pg 147	A way to analyze the personnel of a manager organization (their ownership position, age, experience, and longevity with their firm).
10	Ch 11 Pg 153	A scoreboard to allow you to gauge the compensation levels of key investment personnel (to help you decide whether

Client Guide Number	Page Reference	Value of the Client Guide
		they are likely to remain where they are).
11	Ch 12 Pgs 169–170	Investment management fees for equity and balanced funds—what seems reasonable or exorbitant, along with the "vibrations" that various fees suggest about both manager and client expectations.
11a	Ch 12 Pgs 171–172	Same as Client Guide 11, but for fixed-income accounts.
12	Ch 13 Pg 180	A graphic way of tracking a manager's proficiency at buying and selling securities. Another way of judging managerial qualities.
13	Ch 14 Pg 193	A suggested log for client meetings with managers to ensure that the most important considerations are covered.
14	Ch 15 Pgs 201–204	"Confusing Client Dicta": some typical statements made by clients that may be more dangerous than they sound.
15	Ch 16 Pg 218	"A Minimum Checklist For Manager Assessment": The very least you should expect in information from potential investment advisers you are assessing.

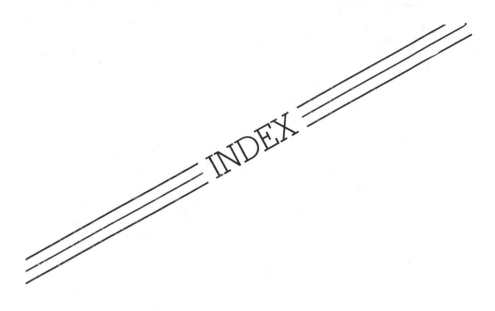